Ethics and the rule of law

Justice and the rule of law

Ethics and the rule of law

DAVID LYONS

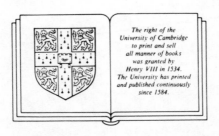

The right of the
University of Cambridge
to print and sell
all manner of books
was granted by
Henry VIII in 1534.
The University has printed
and published continuously
since 1584.

CAMBRIDGE UNIVERSITY PRESS

CAMBRIDGE

NEW YORK   NEW ROCHELLE

MELBOURNE   SYDNEY

Published by the Press Syndicate of the University of Cambridge
The Pitt Building, Trumpington Street, Cambridge CB2 1RP
32 East 57th Street, New York, NY 10022, USA
10 Stamford Road, Oakleigh, Melbourne 3166, Australia

First published 1984
Reprinted 1985 (twice), 1987, 1989

Printed in Great Britain at
The Bath Press, Avon

Library of Congress catalogue card number: 83–7687

British Library Cataloguing in Publication Data

Lyons, David
Ethics and the rule of law.
1. Law and ethics
I. Title
340 '.112   BJ55

ISBN 0 521 25785 9 hard covers
ISBN 0 521 27712 4 paperback

To my father,
and to the memory of my mother

CONTENTS

vii

PREFACE

This book grew out of a variety of courses and seminars I have taught at Cornell University since 1964. These have been exciting times for legal philosophy – sparked by social crises and intellectual adventures. That period is far from over.

And so this book is not a text for a static subject, but a report in progress. It is meant, first of all, for those who wish to become acquainted with contemporary reflections on the nature of law and, especially, its relations to moral reasoning. In that respect it is meant to serve as an introduction to legal philosophy. But it may also interest those who, from the perspective of a single discipline such as law, philosophy, or political science, already have some knowledge of the subject and wish to explore it further, systematically.

I am grateful to Jeremy Mynott of the Cambridge University Press for first suggesting this project to me, and for his patience thereafter. For thoughtful, helpful comments on the draft, I am indebted to Neil MacCormick, William Nelson, and – most especially – David Brink. Judy Oltz and Jylanda Diles produced impeccable typescripts with cheerful efficiency. The Cornell Law School and the Sage School of Philosophy provided time, support, and stimulation.

The book is partial (if symbolic) payment of a debt to those who have most helped me learn about the subject – those who have given me the opportunity to help them learn about it. Next to students, I have learned most from those named in the text – writers, past and present, whose ideas merit the respect of careful study and searching criticism.

Ithaca, April 1983   D.L.

Introduction

Philosophical problems concerning law fall within two broad areas: the fundamental nature of law, and how law may be evaluated. Analytical jurisprudence asks, what is a law, and how is it part of a system? How can a decision be made according to law, when the law is unclear? How is law like and unlike other social norms? How is it like or unlike moral standards?

Normative jurisprudence deals with the appraisal of law and moral issues that law generates. Human law can be made and changed by deliberate decision: what direction should those decisions take? Law claims authority to lay down rules and enforce them: are its claims warranted? Can we legitimately refuse to comply? Things are done in the name of the law which are not normally justifiable: people interfere in others' lives, they deprive others of goods, liberty, even life itself. How, if at all, can such practices be defended?

Analytical and normative questions concerning law are closely connected. The law speaks of rights and responsibility, duties and obligations, fairness, justice, and justification: does this mean that law inevitably contains or satisfies moral standards? Ideas about the essential nature of law have emphasized either its connections with, or else its separation from, morality: which view is right?

This book is an introduction to the philosophy of law. It seeks to explain such questions and to suggest how they may be

1

answered. Meant for the non-specialist, it presupposes neither legal training nor formal study in philosophy. It does not attempt to survey the vast variety of ideas that people have had concerning the nature or appraisal of law. Instead, it addresses such questions by selecting views for discussion that meet the following tests: they are historically important, and their study helps to illuminate the law while making accessible current issues in legal philosophy.

The chapters that follow reflect the dual concern of legal philosophy. Because theories about the nature of law as well as about the direction it should take involve conceptions of morality, we begin, in chapter 1, by considering the nature of moral judgments, and especially their possible justification.

Chapter 2 begins our study of the law itself. It examines the notion that law is a matter of social fact, starting with the familiar idea that laws are commands. These views emphasize the separation of law and morality.

Chapter 3 considers ways in which law, by its very nature, might be connected with morality. It examines legal obligations, the morality of regulating behavior by law, and, especially, the role of moral principles in adjudication.

Chapter 4 examines general theories of evaluation that bear directly on law. It considers how human welfare, rights and obligations, and social justice are relevant to moral judgment. By subjecting normative theories to critical scrutiny, it complements the discussion of justification begun in chapter 1. It also lays the groundwork for dealing with more specific moral problems that arise within a legal context.

Two of the most important and pervasive of these problems are explored in chapters 5 and 6. Some people consider coercion a fundamental feature of the law and it is, in any case, typically found in legal systems. Chapter 5 examines justifications for legal punishment, the law's most familiar method of enforcement. Through its use of coercive regulations, law limits human liberty. Chapter 6 examines bounds that should be placed on legal interference with our free choice.

Chapter 7 takes up "the rule of law" by focusing on two

aspects of that ideal: the values that may be found in legal processes, especially how they relate to the outcomes of legal procedures, and the idea that we all have an obligation to obey the law.

This book is not a survey, neither is it neutral. Like most philosophical studies, its mode of exploration involves both exposition and arguments that are meant to test the soundness of the views discussed. Philosophical ideas are treated seriously when they are subjected to the most demanding critical appraisal. Views that are suggested or defended in this book are, of course, candidates for the same treatment.

It seems only fair to let the reader know what some of those views are, so I shall mention the more persistent ones now. Though law is no simple fact, we have more reason to regard it as a social datum, subject to moral appraisal, than as something automatically informed by moral principles. And, while the claim of moral judgments to objectivity is problematic, we have more reason to regard them as requiring and sometimes enjoying justification, than as groundless, arbitrary, or irremediably subjective.

But a reader need by no means agree with these ideas or take them for granted. Let them be subjected to searching scrutiny, just like the theories that are examined in the chapters that follow.

1

Moral judgment and the law

In our everyday affairs, we judge laws to be good or bad, just or unjust. Our judgments are of practical importance. We consider ways to make law better, and we engage in political activities which range from voting to movements for reform. We discuss these matters with each other and debate them in the political arena.

Our political discussions seem to presuppose that moral judgments are not, or need not be, fundamentally arbitrary. We offer arguments for the positions that we take, and we seek to answer arguments for opposing views. While each of us is likely to have some firm moral convictions, we often recognize that some of our specific judgments might be mistaken. All of this suggests that there are right and wrong answers to moral questions.

But we may come to wonder whether this is really true. Most of us are uncertain about the principles to be used in evaluating law and human conduct generally. We favor freedom, equality, and the common good, but we are unclear about what these ideas mean, how sound principles may be formulated, and even whether any moral standards can rationally be defended.

Our skeptical doubts about morality may be reinforced by reflection on the contrast between science and ethics, a familiar theme in this age of scientific progress. It is often said that science deals with facts, which are outside of us and objective, while ethics is concerned with values, which are in us and subjective. Facts can be observed, or at least they can be verified by empirical techniques. But values (it is said) do not describe the world; they express our wishes, hopes, desires, attitudes, or preferences. They represent the way we want the world to be, not the way it is. We do not find them in but rather impose them on the world. Different individuals and different peoples have differing views about the way the world should be, but none of these, it may be said, can be objectively established. Values are inherited, inculcated, or chosen. Thus, values (it is often said) are at bottom arbitrary.

It seems wise to confront these skeptical doubts about morality directly. For moral issues pervade the study of law. They concern not only the appraisal but also the analysis of law, as many theories about the nature of law stress either its independence from or else its links with morality. We cannot hope to evaluate these views, or even understand them, without becoming clearer about the nature of morality.

That is the aim of this chapter. Our emphasis will be on skeptical challenges to morality. We shall consider a variety of ideas which seem to discredit the notion that moral judgments need not be arbitrary. We cannot hope to exhaust the topic, but we can gain some understanding of what is at stake.

Skeptical challenges are not always limited to morality. General skepticism challenges the possibility of any knowledge whatsoever, including knowledge of the natural world. This raises issues that have puzzled reflective people from time immemorial. Our concerns are more limited. We shall take for granted that we can have knowledge of the world around us and shall consider the more specific skeptical challenges to morality.

We must begin with a comment on the contrast between facts and values. These are not analogous. When values are said to be in us and subjective, one is referring to convictions or beliefs – our beliefs about the values that things have. When facts are said to be outside us and objective, one is referring to states of affairs – aspects of the world that may be the subject of factual beliefs. Moral skepticism may deny that things have value, except insofar as we value them. But it cannot deny that we make evaluations, that we have moral beliefs. For our purposes, then, we should compare beliefs about the world (beliefs that certain facts obtain) with moral beliefs (beliefs about what is good or right or just). We shall assume that factual beliefs can be true or false, right or wrong, sound or unsound. The question posed by moral skepticism is whether moral beliefs can be true or false, right or wrong, sound or unsound.

Law and moral standards

Legal theory has always concerned itself with the nature of morality, as we can see from a brief examination of two classic conceptions of law. Thomas Aquinas and John Austin describe the law in very different terms and seem to approach the study of law in different ways. St Thomas of Aquino (1225–74) was a founder of the "natural law" tradition within jurisprudence, and Austin (1790–1859) helped to establish "legal positivism." Their views are usually contrasted. But they share some common concerns and important similarities lie beneath the surface of their differences. Both writers stressed that law is subject to appraisal from a moral point of view, and both believed that there are standards by which the law may properly be judged.

In his "Treatise on Law," Aquinas says that "Law is nothing else than an ordinance of reason for the common good, promulgated by him who has the care of the community."[1] Aquinas seems to assume that those who make laws wish their subjects well and always establish rules that serve the common good. By contrast, Austin sees the law as a brute social fact based on power, which can be exercised for good or ill. In *The Province of Jurisprudence Determined*, Austin says that "A law is a command which obliges a person or persons ... Laws and other commands are said to proceed from *superiors*, and to bind or oblige *inferiors*." He explains, further, that "the term *superiority* signifies *might*: the power of affecting others with evil and pain, and of forcing them, through fear of that evil, to fashion their conduct to one's wishes."[2] Laws are coercive commands, which can be wise or foolish, just or unjust.

It may seem as if these two theorists disagree fundamentally about the nature of law and its relations to morality. Austin seems more realistic. Experience tells us that law is capable of doing good but also has great potential for evil. It can settle disputes that would otherwise lead to private feuds, provide security, and enhance liberty, but it can be an instrument of oppression, protecting fraud, shrinking liberty, enforcing chattel slavery. Law does not necessarily serve the common good, nor is it always designed to do so.

Aquinas is not blind, however, to these aspects of human law. His general characterization of law, as "an ordinance of reason for the common good," does not automatically apply to what he calls laws "framed by man." These, he says, "are either just or unjust."[3] ". . . the force of a law depends on the extent of its justice . . . according to the rule of reason. But the first rule of reason is the law of nature . . . Consequently, every human law has just so much of the nature of law as it is derived from the law of nature. But if in any point it departs from the law of nature, it is no longer a law but a perversion of law."[4] I understand this to mean that unjust human laws are a perversion of the ideal of law, which is given by right reason and the law of nature.

According to Aquinas, human laws are just when they serve the common good, distribute burdens fairly, show no disrespect for God, and do not exceed the law maker's authority. When laws framed by humans fail to satisfy these conditions, they are unjust. And then, Aquinas says, they do not "bind in conscience." One is morally bound to obey just laws, but not unjust laws. One should obey unjust laws only when circumstances demand it, "in order to avoid scandal or disturbance."[5] Human law does not automatically merit our respect, and its legitimate claim to our obedience depends on moral considerations that are independent of human law.

Austin approaches the study of law somewhat differently. He is concerned to lay the groundwork for professional legal training, and so he wishes to emphasize the distinction between what he calls "positive law" and other standards, including those by which law may properly be judged.[6] This is also necessary, he believes, to insure sound appraisal and intelligent reform of positive law.

Austin provides a general theory about the nature of rules that are supposed to regulate human behavior, which he believes can be understood on the model of coercive commands that create obligations. He first of all distinguishes laws that are meant to describe regularities in the natural world from laws that are meant to guide the behavior of individuals who are capable of modifying their own conduct accordingly. Austin then divides the latter realm into three parts: Divine law, positive law, and positive morality. Divine law consists of the rules for humans that are laid down by God. Positive laws are created by "political superiors," such as the "sovereign" of a community – some person or set of persons habitually obeyed by the bulk of the community and habitually obedient to no other human.[7] Positive morality includes some rules that are explicitly laid down, but also includes some guidelines that are not formally expressed or enforced, but are determined by a convergence of popular attitudes and supported by informal social pressures. Much of "positive morality" is what we might call custom or convention.

Positive law can be judged by either of the other standards, but Austin believes that Divine law is supreme: its obligations are superior to any others. He believes that we cannot have direct knowledge of God's will; but, assuming that God is benevolent, he infers that Divine law is meant to serve "general utility."[8] On Austin's view, positive law can be judged as just or unjust depending on whether it serves the welfare of those affected by it.

So, despite their philosophical differences, Aquinas and Austin appear to share some fundamental ideas about human or positive law. Both believe that human law is morally fallible.

It does not necessarily conform to those standards by which it may properly be judged.

Aquinas and Austin also share a traditional theory about the foundation for moral judgments. They believe Divine law provides morality with its required basis. God is seen as the source of the "moral law." Because they accept this idea of an objective morality, they can also distinguish it from the moral beliefs that people happen to have (what Austin calls positive morality).

A theological conception of the foundation for moral judgments is still widely accepted. It is shared not only by many who believe in the existence of a God but also by many who deny or doubt that a God exists. Some atheists accordingly believe that no foundation is possible for moral judgments, and some agnostics are doubtful whether there are objective moral standards.

But many disagree. Some believers do not regard objective moral standards as dependent on God's will. The philosopher Immanuel Kant (1724–1804), for example, based his theory of morality on an understanding of what it is to be a "rational agent," a being capable of directing his own behavior by reasons. One who acts for reasons is committed, Kant believed, to judging actions in general terms. To act for a reason is to commit oneself to a general principle. Kant argued that the fundamental test of the morality of action is whether one could consistently will that the principle of one's action should become a universal law of human nature (his famous "categorical imperative"). The application of reason to action rather than God is the foundation of Kantian ethics.[9]

And of course many who believe that moral standards can be objectively valid have not been believers in God at all. An apt example is Jeremy Bentham (1748–1832), whose legal and moral theory is otherwise similar to Austin's. Bentham believed that laws should serve the welfare of those they affect, but he did not base this on a belief in God. Bentham held that his "principle of utility" is rationally defensible in its own right.[10] Although his principle is controversial, many who reject it nevertheless agree that objective moral standards do not presuppose the existence of a God.

The category of Divine law in Aquinas and Austin thus represents one form of the more general belief that moral judgments need not be arbitrary. It is a theory about how moral judgments can have a secure foundation.

We will not assume their theory here, nor will we take for granted any particular conception of moral judgments. We need to focus on the general idea that moral judgments can be justified. For this is what we all seem to assume when we subject law to moral appraisal.

Ethical nihilism

When we make moral judgments, we deal with them as if they might be justifiable. Let us now consider some views which suggest that this is mistaken. We shall begin with some arguments that are sometimes taken as showing that moral judgments can have no claim to any sort of objectivity.

Anthropology and social psychology have impressed on us the fact that moral attitudes are acquired through a process of "enculturation." They are "learned." We acquire them while growing up in social groups, and they vary accordingly. They reflect different ways in which groups have accommodated themselves to their environments. Like other aspects of culture, moral attitudes can be viewed as more or less conducive to group survival, but – the argument goes – they cannot be appraised on their own merits. For any standards that we use to evaluate them will simply reflect the values we have acquired in the process of our own enculturation.

The general line of reasoning just sketched may be understood as follows. Moral attitudes are the natural outcome of certain natural processes, and this is supposed to show that they cannot enjoy objective validity. We are caused to have the attitudes that we have, which therefore lie outside the realm of reasoning. They are not proper candidates for either truth or falsity.

But does this follow? If the general strategy of argument

were sound, then the same would be true of all our beliefs, not just our moral attitudes – beliefs about the character of the world around us as well as beliefs about how we should conduct ourselves within it. For it seems reasonable to suppose that all our beliefs are likewise acquired, and that they are all the natural products of some natural processes. Scientific beliefs are no exception. We question, investigate, and make claims to knowledge not only *about* but also *within* the web of cause and effect. This line of reasoning would fail to distinguish moral attitudes from any other convictions.

By the same token, this challenge to morality is also self-defeating. If it applies to any beliefs at all, it concerns all beliefs, and so it applies to those expressed within it. One who rejected morality on such grounds would be committed to holding that this reasoning itself, the theories underlying it, and the conclusions drawn from it all lack objective validity. To see what may be wrong with such a line of argument, it is helpful to distinguish between the fact that something is believed and the content of that belief. We can distinguish, for example, between the fact that quantum mechanics arose and has come to enjoy widespread acceptance among physicists, on the one hand, and what quantum mechanics claims, on the other. In a similar way, we can distinguish between the fact that certain ideas about fairness are widely accepted and what those ideas about fairness claim. The study of how beliefs arise and change does not automatically undermine the contents of beliefs or their claims to objectivity. The question that must be faced is what grounds there are for the beliefs. One cannot show that moral beliefs lack objective standing by showing merely that their acceptance can be explained. The question is whether there is something special about them, the way they are acquired or their content, which is sufficient to distinguish them from other beliefs and renders them groundless. The first line of reasoning ignores this question entirely.

If we assume that beliefs about the nature of the world can be true or false, then we may try to contrast these with moral judgments. The feature of scientific beliefs that is usually taken to be relevant is their "testability": they make a reasonable claim to objectivity because they are capable of being tested against experience. This makes scientific judgments capable of being true or false. Moral judgments are sometimes said to be different: they do not describe the world but rather "prescribe" or "evaluate." They do not state what is supposed to be the case but go beyond the facts. They are not testable by observation or experience.

The argument assumes, however, too simple a view of both scientific and moral judgment. Scientific claims of any importance typically go beyond observation in significant ways. A scientific law states a universal relationship between events of certain types, such as the release of an unsupported body within a gravitational field and its reaching a certain velocity. Such a law has implications about the past, present, and future that will never be experienced by anyone, and is established by considerations that do not entail it, because it is much more general than any particular set of actual observations. It cannot be verified conclusively. Nor can discredited scientific hypotheses be conclusively falsified, since their testing involves auxiliary hypotheses and assumptions about test conditions that themselves are not conclusively verified. Scientific laws necessarily exceed actual observations – a fact about them that explains their utility as well as their theoretical fascination. Unless they went beyond actual observations they would not widen our knowledge of the world.

The same is true of claims about so-called "theoretical entities," such as subatomic particles and DNA molecules. The very existence of such entities, which play a major role in natural science, is not directly or conclusively established by observation. Proofs of their existence and their properties rely on complex techniques, such as particle acceleration and X-ray diffraction, and extrapolate well beyond observable facts.

These features of developed science give rise to philosophic theories about the nature of scientific discoveries, some of which seek to "reduce" the content of science to what can be directly observed. But those theories about science should not

be confused with scientific findings, and they compete with
theories that seek to explain how we can learn about features
of the world that go beyond direct observation.

So part of the simple contrast between scientific and moral
beliefs is untenable, since scientific beliefs typically go beyond
observable facts. On the other side, moral judgments are not
completely independent of empirical facts or observation.
Consider my judgment that John's breaking his promise to
Mary was reprehensible. This can be discredited by reference
to the facts – if, say, there was no John or no Mary, John never
made a promise to Mary, Mary tricked John into making it, or
John never broke the promise.

Someone might try to preserve the idea that moral
judgments go beyond the facts by claiming that my judgment
does not merely describe what happened but pronounces a
verdict on it. It may be said, for example, that my judgment
presupposes a general principle of some sort, such as the
principle that breaking a promise is reprehensible. And this, it
may be claimed, cannot be established by appeal to observation. This reply assumes, however, that moral principles
cannot be established on the basis of facts (not even facts about
the human condition). But while that is an important
philosophic theory about morality, it is not an observable fact
about it. And there are competing theories on the other side,
which seek to show how moral principles can be decided by
reference to facts about the human condition. The question
that we face, once more, is whether this is possible. The simple
contrast initially suggested between science and ethics fails to
answer that question.

The simple contrast also makes dubious assumptions; for
example, that rationally respectable beliefs must be testable by
ordinary observation and must be either true or false. Both of
these assumptions can be questioned. Mathematical statements, for example, are not tested by observation. And some
statements which are neither true nor false appear perfectly
respectable. Imperatives, for example, are neither true nor
false, but they are not regarded as inherently arbitrary for that

(not governed by principal)

reason. While some commands are arbitrary, others are perfectly reasonable. This is important because one contrast that is sometimes drawn between moral and other judgments turns on the idea that moral judgments, like imperatives, are intended to guide choices. But this does not show that moral judgments are inherently arbitrary, since we have no reason to assume that the guidance of choices is inherently arbitrary. It is also worth noting that moral judgments are not unique in being used to guide choices. The same is done by legal and prudential statements, which are not regarded as inherently arbitrary. The same is also done by statements of empirical fact. We not only inform but also routinely advise and warn others by telling them facts, such as that the ice on the pond is thin or that the bull is loose in the pasture.

Let us take our bearings. Moral appraisal of the law, like moral judgment in general, typically assumes that a meaningful distinction can be made between sound and unsound moral judgments. Because moral judgments seem to presuppose some general grounds for moral appraisals, it is natural to think that sound moral judgments (if there are any) presuppose "objective" moral principles. We have been discussing the more general idea that moral judgments might be sound, *whatever* their foundation. We can discuss this somewhat independently of the idea that there are "objective" moral standards, just as we can entertain the idea that scientific judgments might be sound without assuming any particular theory about the foundations of science. Our discussion has not shown that moral judgments are rationally respectable, but it has shown that certain familiar dismissals of morality are ill-considered.

Social relativism

It is a commonplace of modern thought that morality is "relative to culture." But these words can refer to several different, somewhat independent ideas about morality, which we need to sort out and examine carefully.

Let us begin with an idea that has already been mentioned. If our values are shaped initially by a process of social conditioning, then any given person is likely to form moral judgments which accord with the values that are frequently found within her social group. The judgments we make, as we begin to appraise conduct and institutions, are likely to reflect the attitudes that have influenced the development of our own values. But the process is complex, and its effects should not be oversimplified. We are subject to many cultural influences, and prevailing attitudes evolve. The values we initially acquire can conflict when they are applied, and tensions can arise among our moral attitudes. We may find, for example, that our concern for others' welfare conflicts with the value that we place on individual freedom, and we may face a dilemma when others resent our efforts to help them. We may then act without reflection, following our more firmly held values; or we may try to decide which are more important. In this way, we can begin to shape our own moral convictions.

Furthermore, an awareness of social conditioning can make me less dogmatic in my moral attitudes. And I may find that those around me tend to make moral judgments which cannot survive critical scrutiny because they embody false beliefs, neglect of human interests, or unjustifiable notions of superiority. One whose attitudes have been influenced by Hollywood films, for example, may initially think of Native Americans as alien savages who have properly been dispossessed, but may later come to believe that the original Americans have rights which for generations have been systematically violated.

So, while our values will continue somewhat to reflect the attitudes of those around us, we find ourselves increasingly capable of rejecting conventional moral judgments. We recognize that prevailing standards are subject to criticism.

Suppose that I live in a society in which it is generally accepted that wives should defer to the wishes of their husbands. Wives are supposed to live the kinds of lives their husbands choose, raise children in the way their husbands wish, and accept their husbands' sexual demands. Suppose, however, that I can see no justification for the subordination of one spouse to the other and believe that wives and husbands have equal rights to each other's consideration and respect. My moral opinion is not to be discounted just because it is unconventional. Conventional morality can sensibly be challenged. To accept this, we do not need to assume that my nonconforming moral judgment is correct. I can recognize that it might be mistaken, for I need not be dogmatic. But neither must I regard prevailing standards as sound. Morality is not "relative to culture" in that way.

This point is vital to an understanding of the problem of ethnocentrism, the tendency to evaluate practices found in other social groups by the dogmatic application of one's own society's values. Social scientists have long been interested in the phenomenon of cultural diversity. In different groups one finds variations in sexual and child-rearing practices, in marital arrangements and kinship patterns, in modes of economic and political organization, which are accompanied by values that differ from one's own. Ethnocentrism interferes with the sensitive observation of other groups' practices and with an appreciation of the many ways in which societies can be organized to serve human needs. To conduct effective social research, one must first of all be able to detach oneself, to some degree, from the values of the society to which one belongs. One cannot be morally dogmatic.

Furthermore, social research is not conducted in a vacuum. Nations have built empires by subjugating other groups, and this process has been reinforced by ethnocentric attitudes – the idea that we can export "civilization" by imposing our social system on other peoples. It is understandable, then, that social scientists have often been outspoken critics of colonial practices and cultural prejudices. Many have become champions of human rights, including the rights of other nations to self-determination, to mutual respect, and tolerance.

The moral attitudes thus expressed are by no means "relativistic." They involve the idea that people throughout the world have some identical basic rights, and more generally the idea that certain fundamental principles apply to all people in all places at all times. There is nothing relativistic in this.

What *seems* relativistic is the associated notion that there may be equally good, just, and morally defensible ways of organizing human affairs. Not only are our own ways subject to criticism, but others' ways may be well adapted to the needs of the people who are affected.

But if we dig beneath the surface relativism of this notion, we can see that it involves more fundamental values which are by no means "relative." Social organization should serve human needs and respect people's rights, for example. The rejection of ethnocentrism does not imply that "anything goes," but is meant to make us more appreciative of the varied ways in which human needs may, or may fail to be, served.

Sometimes, however, those who say that morality is "relative to culture" express themselves in ways that seem to mean something much more radical. For example, the American sociologist William Graham Sumner (1840–1910) wrote that "the mores can make anything right."[11] As the mores of a group are simply standards that are generally accepted within the group, this seems to say that positive or conventional morality always determines which acts are right and which are wrong. Sumner seemed to confirm this when he claimed that "immoral" *means* "conflicts with the mores."[12] If that were true, the only proper basis for moral appraisals would be standards that are widely accepted. Believing would make it so – provided that enough people happen to agree.

Though claims of this sort once were common in social science, it is unclear that the writers meant exactly what they seemed to be saying. Nevertheless, their writings do suggest an important theory about morality.

Let us call a theory like Sumner's "social relativism." Its implications may be illustrated in the following way. Suppose that Alice has had an abortion. On the theory under consideration, Alice's having an abortion was immoral if, and only if, having an abortion is condemned by the mores of the group. If the mores condemn abortion, her act was wrong; if they do not condemn abortion, her act was not wrong. The mores might discriminate between abortions under different circumstances; but that complication makes no difference here. On this theory, the mores make Alice's act, and all other acts, right or wrong.

Actually, the theory as so far stated (and as presented by those who appear to endorse it) is to some extent unclear, since it fails to acknowledge two complicating factors: people usually belong to more than one social group at any given time; and moral judgments can be made of conduct performed by members of other groups. The resulting complications are important.

Even within relatively simple societies, people belong to different social classes, kinship groups, and groups determined by the social division of labor. More complex societies contain a myriad of smaller subcommunities, churches, and voluntary organizations. If (as social relativism assumes) definite moral attitudes can be ascribed to social groups, they can be ascribed to many of the groups mentioned. And, most important, one can simultaneously belong to distinct groups with different norms, or prevailing moral standards. Alice, for example, may belong to a church that condemns abortion and yet be a member of a family, peer group, or voluntary organization that condones it. How, according to the theory under consideration, should Alice's conduct be judged? According to the norms of just one of these groups, or according to the norms of all of them? Neither approach seems satisfactory.

To simplify matters, one might be tempted to interpret the theory in the first way suggested, as saying that Alice's conduct should be judged by the norms of *just one* of the groups to which she belongs. But which one should it be? If she really belongs to more than one social group, the theory cannot pretend that Alice belongs to just one. No adequate theory can be built upon a fiction. But if one wishes to judge Alice's conduct by the norms of just one social group when she may belong to more than one, then the most natural approach to identifying one would be to say that Alice's conduct should be judged by the norms of a group whose norms she endorses. But note what this amounts to: <u>Alice's conduct should be judged by norms that *she herself* accepts</u>. To interpret the theory in this way is not to develop social relativism so much as to forsake it. Social relativism holds that membership in a social group has decisive moral significance. But on this interpretation of the theory only Alice's *personal* values are accorded that significance. The result would be a form of individualistic relativism, which we shall turn to later.

The other possible way of dealing with multiple group membership is to interpret the theory as saying that Alice's conduct should be judged by the norms of *each* of the groups to which she belongs. This shows how social relativism is capable of endorsing conflicting moral judgments. For, if we judge Alice's conduct on the basis of her church's norms, then we must condemn her action, and if we also judge her conduct on the basis of her family's norms, then we must condone her action.

But does this make good sense? On the surface, "Alice's having an abortion was wrong" appears logically incompatible with "Alice's having an abortion was not wrong." If the theory endorses both judgments, it would not be liberal and openminded: it would be incoherent. It would endorse contradictions, like "It is raining (here and now)" and "It is not raining (here and now)." Any theory that endorses contradictions insures that it has false implications, which insures it is mistaken.

This fatal embarrassment can be avoided if we suppose that the two conflicting judgments which the theory is committed to endorsing are not really incompatible. Moral judgments might be taken as implicitly referring to the norms of particular groups, so that what is really meant when it is said that Alice's having an abortion is wrong is that her act conflicts with the norms of a particular social group, and what is really meant when it is said that her having an abortion is not wrong is that her act does *not* conflict with the norms of a *different* group. But this is implausible. One's moral judgment may be influenced by group norms, but when one judges Alice's act one does not refer to those norms. Nor is one committed to regarding them as moral authorities.

An alternative way of trying to make the two conflicting judgments appear compatible is by claiming that neither is to be regarded as simply true or false, that a judgment is only "true for" those who belong to the group whose norms are reflected in the judgment. But this does not really help. For what can it mean to say that a judgment is "true for" a particular person or group? The most plausible interpretation of this form of speech is that it means the judgment is *believed* or *accepted* by those individuals. And that is not what is at stake. The question is whether Alice's having an abortion *is wrong*. We acknowledge that people can disagree about this, that they can accept conflicting judgments of a given act. This proposal brings us back to where we started.

Social relativism's endorsement of conflicting moral judgments is not, however, the only difficulty that it faces. The theory is ambiguous in another important way. The person whose conduct is being judged may belong to a group to which the person who is judging her conduct does not belong.

Let us suppose, for example, that we who are judging Alice's conduct belong to none of the groups in which she can claim membership. For simplicity's sake, let us ignore the added complication we have just been discussing and suppose that Alice belongs to just one social group, which condemns her abortion, while the norms of our group do not condemn it. Which way does the theory say that we should judge her act?

This second complication is like the first in that it shows how the theory can find itself endorsing contradictory moral judgments. But there is another lesson to be learned from this particular complication. We can imagine two distinct ways of developing relativistic theories, depending on whether we focus on the *agent* (the one whose conduct is being judged) or the *appraiser* (the one judging the conduct). An agent-based version of social relativism would hold that a person's conduct must be judged by the norms of the group to which she (the agent) belongs. That is the way we have taken social relativism so far. But there seems as much reason to hold that group norms are relevant to the moral *judgments* that one might make as there is to hold that they are relevant to the *actions* one performs. An appraiser-based version of social relativism would say that a person's moral judgment is sound if, and only if, it accords with the norms of that person's (the appraiser's) social group.

These two variations on social relativism give us differing instructions for judging conduct. According to the agent-based theory, the morality of Alice's act depends on the norms of her group, but according to the appraiser-based theory it depends on the norms of the appraiser's group. Since we are assuming that the norms of different groups can differ, and since agents and appraisers can belong to different groups, it makes a difference which version of the theory we apply. But neither seems more plausible than the other.

Our discussion of social relativism has suggested some of the difficulties that must be overcome by any theory of this type. But the basic point common to all forms of social relativism is that conduct must be judged by conventionally accepted or prevailing moral standards. This is their distinctive feature, and also the source of all their difficulties. Let us look once more at that general idea.

The question that we face may be put as follows: does it make sense to judge conduct independently of group norms? If so, and if such judgments may not be automatically discredited, then social relativism is essentially misguided. That seems to be the case.

Social groups are not simple, homogeneous collections of individuals who agree about everything. Real social groups not only differ from one another but also encompass diversity among their own members. While the members of a single group can be assumed to share some important values, they often disagree on some moral issues. It takes no stretch of the imagination – it requires no science fiction story – for us to suppose that Alice's sincere judgment about her abortion might differ from the judgment accepted by most other members of some group to which she belongs. According to the sort of theory we have been considering, Alice's judgment counts for nothing, however, unless it happens to agree with the standards that are generally accepted in some social group – *regardless* of what she might have to say about the *merits* of her case. According to this sort of theory, the only merit of a moral judgment and of the conduct it concerns is its agreement with some group's norms. This shows that social relativism entails the most extreme form of moral conventionalism that is possible. It endorses the position of the moral majority and automatically discounts minority moral opinion on all subjects.

But we have no reason to discount the moral judgment of individuals who happen to disagree with group norms. We have no reason to believe that moral judgment is sound if, and only if, it happens to coincide with majority sentiment, or that conduct cannot be moral unless it conforms to conventional morality. Social relativism therefore does not seem an enlightened conception of morality. It does not even seem to represent conventional ideas about morality!

This is not to say that established social norms merit no respect. It has often been claimed, for example, that one has an obligation to conform to the established rules of one's social group, including – most importantly – its laws. Why should we believe this? It may be said that conformity to established rules is vital to the welfare of the group or that, in view of the benefits one derives from others' compliance with those rules when others would rather deviate from them, one owes it in fairness to others to comply with the rules when one's own turn comes.

All such arguments for obedience to established social rules differ from social relativism in the following respect: they do not treat established rules or social norms as the basic standards for moral appraisal. All such arguments assume some more general reason why established rules should be obeyed, such as promoting the welfare of the group or acting fairly towards others. These reasons are not treated as if they were "relative" to specific cultures. In other words, such arguments assume some *universal* principle of obligation. What such an obligation may require one to do depends on circumstances that vary, as established rules vary from one society to another, and in this respect the idea of such an obligation has "relativistic" overtones. But the underlying principle is not assumed to vary or to be relative to culture.

No less important is the fact that the familiar arguments seeking to show that we are under an obligation to obey established rules cannot be taken as implying an absolute, unqualified, or universal obligation to conform. Suppose, for example, that exploitation of a slave is permitted by law or by other social norms within a community. It cannot be assumed that the welfare of the community always depends on the continued subservience of a slave or that fairness always requires that a slave comply with laws that permit her exploitation by others. In some cases, at least, these conditions will *not* be satisfied. So, even if it were true that one is under an obligation to obey established rules whenever compliance serves the welfare of the community or whenever fairness to others requires it, we could not infer that one always has an obligation to conform.

To the extent that there is an obligation to conform to established social rules, the morality of specific types of act will be "relative to culture." Culture, which includes established social rules, will make a difference to what it is morally permissible to do. This is because it may be harmful, say, or unfair, to neglect established rules. Or it may be insensitive and hurtful to do so, even if the rules have little to commend them. Thus, it may be wrong to ignore the practices of those around one, just because it may offend them needlessly or show lack of respect for their values. In a similar way, it may be wrong to drive on a particular side of the road, not because such an act is inherently wrong (or even dangerous in the circumstances), but simply because there is adequate justification for respecting the more or less arbitrary laws of the community.

The discussion so far has suggested that there are several ways in which morality can be "relative to culture." Nothing suggested so far, however, would allow us to infer that the morality of conduct or institutions is simply a matter of conformity to prevailing values. Quite the contrary.

Individualistic relativism

Our discussion has suggested the legitimacy of unconventional moral judgments. It might lead one to suspect that moral values are fundamentally matters for individual choice or decision.

There is some truth in this idea. While values can be ascribed to groups, that is because they are held by those within the groups. Individuals make moral judgments. Individuals have and express moral opinions. But this does not mean that individuals' moral opinions are self-certifying. For all we can tell so far, moral beliefs may, like other beliefs, be true or false, correct or incorrect, sound or unsound.

Relativistic theories about morality do not reject these alternative possibilities. They claim neither that all moral judgments are sound nor that none are. Social relativism claims that moral judgments are sound just when they accord with the values of some group or other. Individualistic forms of relativism, by contrast, rest on the idea that moral judgments are sound just when the individuals who make them satisfy certain conditions that may or may not be satisfied.

Some atheistic existentialists seem to embrace this sort of theory. Beginning with the assumption that only a God could provide the basis for objective moral principles, but unwilling to reject morality along with the idea that God exists, they conclude that moral principles are products of human existence which are properly regulated by individual decision. If we are to be responsible, to avoid an "inauthentic" existence, such writers hold, we must face the issue squarely, decide deliberately what values we are prepared to endorse, and *choose* them for ourselves. Then we can judge responsibly.

Not only existentialists have regarded moral principles in

such a light. Others hold that moral principles "prescribe" the way we wish the world to be, as opposed to describing what it is like. Because principles do not describe the world, they can neither correspond nor fail to correspond to objective facts and therefore cannot be established as objectively binding. We are, however, capable of choosing principles reflectively and with self-awareness. If we choose them responsibly, with due regard to the commitments that we shall be making, then we can apply them responsibly, and the moral judgments our principles support can be regarded as thoroughly justified. They possess no interpersonal validity, but they are not arbitrary either.

Individual relativists do not assume that everyone accepts the same basic values or would do so upon reflection. This sort of theory is therefore relativistic because it in effect endorses a variety of moral positions. It also presents us with the ambiguity that we found in social relativism. Is the idea to be that one's own *conduct* may properly be judged only by standards that one responsibly accepts? Or is it to be that one's moral *judgments* are sound just when they accord with moral principles that one responsibly accepts? The former yields an agent-based theory and the latter an appraiser-based theory, which are not equivalent.

An agent-based individualistic theory says that each individual determines the standards by which she may properly be judged, while an appraiser-based theory says that one must judge according to the standards one accepts. The differences between these versions of individualistic relativism concern judgments made of *other* people's conduct. An agent-based theory tells us, in effect, that a person's conduct can be judged in just one way, and that no one can properly question another person's action so long as it conforms to the agent's values. An appraiser-based theory tells us, in effect, that a person's conduct can soundly be judged in as many ways as people are capable of judging it by reference to their own reflective principles. An agent-based theory sees the moral world as divided into independent individual realms, while an appraiser-based theory yields a moral Tower of Babel.

Instead of pursuing these complications of individualistic relativism further, it may be useful to focus on its notion of justification. A moral judgment is held to be justifiable relative to a decision that an individual might make. Up to a point at least, this may seem perfectly reasonable. But consider the contrast between justified and sound beliefs in other contexts. It may be reasonable for one who has lived all her life on the land and who has developed a reliable sense of weather patterns to make a prediction that disagrees with the responsible forecast made by an expert meteorologist. Though they differ, both individuals might have justified beliefs about the weather, because their beliefs can be based on very good (though not infallible) grounds for making predictions. But they cannot both be right. It is possible to be justified in believing something that turns out to be false, just as it is possible for one to have a belief that is unjustified (because it is based, say, on a guess), but which turns out to be true. Justification is a property of believing, while truth is a property of the content of a belief. According to our ordinary assumptions about moral beliefs, the same distinction applies to them.

But individual relativists seem to hold that moral beliefs can be justified though they are incapable of being true. This is how we must understand appraiser-based versions of individualistic relativism. Suppose that Alice and Barbara have differing reflective views about abortion, so that on this theory their conflicting judgments of Alice's abortion are both to be regarded as justified. It would make no sense for the relativist to hold, in addition, that both beliefs are true. For, if Alice's belief were true, then it would follow that her act was not wrong, and if Barbara's conflicting belief were true, then it would follow that Alice's act was wrong. But it does not make sense to say that Alice's act was both wrong and not wrong. So it does not make sense to suppose that their differing moral beliefs are both true. If the relativist wishes to make sense, he must mean that moral judgments can be justified but cannot be true.

What can it mean to say that a belief is justified if it could not be true? The answer given by an individual relativist is that a moral belief is justified if it can be supported, with the aid of true factual beliefs, by principles that can be ascribed to some individual. But the support given a belief by a principle is only as good as the principle itself. One can therefore appreciate why individual relativists do not regard moral principles as justified if they are held without critical reflection. It is vital that individual relativists have a conception of when acceptance of a moral principle can be justified. Generally speaking, individual relativists believe that acceptance of a principle is justified when it is freely given, with full awareness of what the acceptance commits one to. The test is psychological; it reveals deep-seated values of the individual (which may themselves be influenced by the process of reflection). The question then arises, whether the reflective willingness of an individual to endorse a principle provides the principle with the capacity to justify moral judgments.

Suppose we ask whether it is relevant to the morality of a law or an individual's action that it causes avoidable suffering. An individual relativist must say that such a factor is relevant *only relative to* some individual's reflective choice of moral principles. This implies that there is nothing in itself wrong with causing avoidable suffering; there is no general reason to regard conduct or laws with such effects as bad. It is up to individuals to decide and, of course, different individuals are free to decide differently.

This explains why such a theory appears incapable of dealing with the main concerns of moral judgment in a social context: how to evaluate conduct and institutions when the conflicting interests and divergent convictions of many individuals are at stake. An agent-based version of individualistic relativism implies, for example, that a person may act in *any* way she wishes, so long as she is faithful to her own reflective convictions. It accepts as morally permissible *whatever* one person is, on reflection, willing to do to others. This is a liberal theory indeed – but not very considerate of others who are adversely affected by our actions. According to this sort of theory, no one can justly complain of bad treatment from another person, if the other person acts conscientiously.

An agent-based theory also excludes appraisals of other matters. Some of the things that we wish to judge are not agents, and so they cannot be judged by the values they accept. Such a theory provides no basis for judging social rules, laws, or institutions. It seems an impoverished conception of morality.

Appraiser-based versions of individualistic relativism, by contrast, allow for the possibility of judging social rules, laws, and institutions, but they provide no determinate way of judging them, unless everyone happens to agree – which would be surprising in important and controversial cases. Such a theory accepts the conflicting judgments conscientiously made by individuals, but offers no way of adjudicating moral disputes. It does not tell us, for example, that disputes must be settled fairly, with due regard for each person's legitimate claims, since any requirement of fairness or of respect for legitimate claims is, according to the theory, entirely contingent on the values we reflectively embrace. If I do not care about fairness, then my judgments cannot be faulted for lacking any such concern, and there is nothing more to be said from a moral point of view.

This does not prove that such a theory is mistaken. In evaluating such a theory, however, we must consider whether it seems reasonable to accept the implications of the theory or the opposing view. It seems to me the contest is onesided.

The justification of moral judgments

The several theories of morality we have been considering – from ethical nihilism to individualistic relativism – have little to commend them. The arguments that seem to support them, when any are available, are exceedingly weak. They therefore give us little or no reason to accept their implausible implications. They give us little or no reason to suppose that moral judgments are inherently unsound or that they must be based on variable social norms or individual decisions.

Furthermore, if we think that moral judgments can be used to evaluate not just individual conduct but also social norms, laws, and institutions, we are unlikely to be satisfied with such theories.

These remarks provide no conclusive refutation of either nihilism or relativism (though the versions of such theories that endorse contradictions are self-refuting). Our critical examination of these theories suggests what is at stake in our reflections about the nature of moral judgments, but they do not prove that nihilism or relativism must be rejected. This may seem unsatisfactory. It might be understood to show that moral theory is a pointless exercise that proves nothing. But this would be the wrong lesson to draw.

One reason we cannot conclusively reject either nihilism or relativism is that we have considered only sample forms of such theories. Other forms may be more strongly supported and might have more plausible implications. They might have sufficient support to justify their seemingly unacceptable implications.

But the general sketch of such theories that we have given seems to suggest that they are untenable positions. Why, then, do they persist? One likely explanation involves misplaced expectations about the nature of inquiry into such issues – expectations suggested by the desire for conclusive proofs or refutations. An important conception of knowledge, which one finds throughout the history of philosophy, retains a strong hold on our thinking about morality. The general idea is this. If we have any knowledge at all, it must rest on some things that are certain, that could not possibly be otherwise. Applied to ethics, this conception of knowledge implies that, if we have any moral knowledge at all, it must be based on certain knowledge of undeniable general principles or else must be built up from certain knowledge that we obtain of what is right or wrong, good or bad, just or unjust in particular cases. Such knowledge is not derived from ordinary experience. So, if we have any moral knowledge at all, it must be derived from some mysterious faculty of "moral intuition."

Now, both moral principles and specific moral judgments have sometimes been regarded as "self-evident," but it has never been clear what such a claim amounts to, beyond the expression of subjective confidence. Some philosophers have thought that we possess a special faculty that delivers infallible moral insight, but most of us are unable to receive those messages, those who have claimed to receive them disagree about their contents, and the nature of the faculty has never been explained. The very idea of such a faculty seems absurd. If the idea of moral knowledge rests on such assumptions, it too must be untenable.

Before we draw such conclusions, however, we should examine the general conception of knowledge that this view of ethics assumes. This way of thinking implies that all knowledge of the world around us can be derived from rationally undeniable principles about the nature of the world or else must be built up, step by indubitable step, from a variety of particular truths, such as those we learn from simple, incorrigible observation. If we take this seriously, however, we must conclude that we have little knowledge of the world. Almost all that we have thought we gained from science, for example, must be illusory. Scientific progress does not rest on indubitable truths. Nor could it do so, since we have no special faculty delivering insight about the general laws of nature, and our knowledge of those laws always goes beyond specific observations that we have made or ever could make.

Science is not infallible. The understanding that it gives us is subject to correction, when good reasons are found to modify established beliefs. But our experience seems to show that scientific progress is not illusory. Our increased understanding of the world, however limited it may be, is shown by our increased ability to affect what goes on within the natural order. If we accept this modest notion of scientific progress, therefore, we have to give up the ancient notion that knowledge rests on indubitable foundations.

This suggests that we demand too much of ethics if we expect absolute proof of general principles or indisputable certification of specific moral judgments. In this area of life, as in any other, we are seeking good reasons for one moral position as opposed to others, if such can be found.

Our examination of ethical nihilism and relativism suggests that there are good reasons *against* such conceptions of morality. As we proceed, we shall consider some moral theories of importance in a political context, which do not regard moral judgments as inherently arbitrary or merely relative to culture or individual decisions. An example is utilitarianism. We shall subject the principle of utility to critical appraisal. We shall find neither a conclusive proof nor a conclusive refutation of that principle, but we shall consider some arguments for it as well as arguments against it. To the extent that we find reasons to accept such a principle, we shall have reason to believe that moral judgments are not inherently arbitrary.

It is sometimes suggested that the procedures we use in appraising moral principles are fruitless because they involve arguing in a circle. General principles have specific implications, so we appraise principles in terms of their implications for particular cases. And specific judgments seem to require support from general principles, so we appraise particular judgments by considering what principles could be used to justify them. But this seems like moving in a circle. The most that such a mode of argument can establish is the consistency or inconsistency of a moral position. But equally consistent positions can disagree, so this mode of argument cannot settle any moral disputes.

But this would be too hasty. First, this argumentative strategy seems to imply that moral judgments are subject to the same logical constraints and operations, such as consistency and implication, that regulate other judgments. Moral positions can be discredited if they are internally inconsistent. This is not a small claim to make in the face of ethical nihilism, which seems to imply that moral judgments lie entirely outside the realm of reason and are not regulated by logical principles.

Second, as the argumentative strategy implies, moral

judgments work at different levels, such as general principles and specific judgments. The implications of a general principle for specific cases depends on matters of fact. The support of a specific judgment by a general principle depends on matters of fact. Facts, or assumptions about them, are relevant in several ways. Many of the judgments that we make reflect our ignorance or misapprehensions about the facts, our failure to appreciate the full range of interests that are at stake, and the full impact of decisions on those interests. Both specific judgments and general principles can be discredited to the extent that they rest on mistaken assumptions of fact. This means that we do not simply work within a circle of moral judgments. Some moral judgments can be discounted on empirical grounds. More generally, our moral attitudes cannot be taken in isolation, but must be fitted into a systematic collection of beliefs which include beliefs about the world around us, human nature, and the consequences of decisions.

Furthermore, many moral disagreements do not reflect differences of principle at all but rather disputes about the facts. Good examples are unfortunately provided by government decisions, such as the decision to make war. History shows that governments often falsify or distort the facts in order to justify military actions that they wish to take. The escalation of US military involvement in Vietnam was justified, for example, by false governmental claims about an incident in the Gulf of Tonkin. Even now, those who disagree about the justifiability of US military involvement in Southeast Asia disagree less about the fundamentals of political morality than about a variety of facts, such as the effects of such involvement on the populations of that region.

The relevant facts can be much more controversial than the moral judgments. Consider an example. Suppose a moral theory T holds that an act is to be judged by the pleasure and pain it produces: the more pleasure, the better it is; the more pain, the worse it is; and acts should be chosen so that they produce as much net pleasure (subtracting pain) or as little net pain as possible. According to this view, any pleasure caused by an act tends to justify it.

Note, then, what theory T implies about rape. If a rapist derives pleasure from his act, that tends to justify the act – it provides a positive argument for performing it. If the pleasure that the act of rape gives the rapist happens to be greater than the pain that it causes, then the rape is justifiable, at least if no more pleasure can be derived from any alternative act open to the rapist. But is this plausible?

We are almost certainly ignorant of just how much pain or pleasure is caused by a given act of rape and yet we can be confident in the judgment that rape cannot be justified in such terms, if it can be justified at all. The idea that rape is wrong seems much more certain than the theory under consideration or the facts about pleasure and pain produced in particular cases. And the claim that rape is wrong is not insupportable. Although the pleasure it occasions appears morally irrelevant, the pain it causes is surely not. The act furthermore involves a brutal, if only temporary, domination of one person by another. It manifests the desire to impose one's will on another, and it imposes a sense of powerlessness on the victim, in addition to the violation itself. Between man and woman, the act of rape symbolizes and reinforces a pattern of domination that transcends the individual act – a pattern of treatment and training that not only discriminates but also shrivels hopes and crushes aspirations.

These reflections do not suggest merely that such a theory is unacceptable but also that we can make claims to moral knowledge that are at least as valid as the claims we make about the world around us. If someone doubts this, he might try to defend a form of moral skepticism. But our experience so far suggests that nihilism and relativism have much more dubious foundations than the judgment that rape is wrong.

If someone wishes to challenge that judgment, he needs to show that the factors cited are irrelevant or illusory. If his arguments fail, then our judgment, which is not groundless to begin with, will have an even greater claim to being sound, because it will have resisted challenges. If his arguments advance our understanding of what is at stake, then he will have increased our moral knowledge. For our moral knowledge, just like our knowledge of other matters, depends on how our judgments fit together and can be reinforced by further experience. That is the standard for knowledge in the rest of our lives. We can ask for no less here.

2

Law as social fact

Our focus now shifts from morality to law. Although reflection about the nature of law goes back to ancient times, it is useful to begin our study of legal theory with the ideas presented by John Austin in the last century. For Austin provides one of the first highly developed theories of law, which incorporates both ideas about law and more general philosophical assumptions whose influence remains quite strong today.

Austin was influenced most directly by Bentham, whose theory of law was spurred by eighteenth-century movements for codification and reform of law. As codification requires the replacement of somewhat independent judicial decisions on specific cases by a systematic code of laws, Bentham was drawn into legal philosophy because he wished to base his codification proposals on an understanding of law's basic elements. But Bentham's principal analytic study, *Of Laws in General*, though completed in the eighteenth century, was not published until recently,[13] so it had much less influence on the development of jurisprudence than Austin's more familiar works. Austin's writings set the stage for contemporary jurisprudential controversies.

As we have seen, Austin develops his theory of law within the framework of a more general theory of norms governing human conduct. Any law "properly so called," whether made by God or humans, is "a rule laid down for the guidance of an intelligent being by an intelligent being having power over him."[14] Laws "properly so called" are commands, which are attributable to individuals who are able and willing to impose sanctions in case of noncompliance. Jurisprudence is primarily concerned with what Austin calls "positive" laws, which are distinguished from "Divine law" and "positive morality" by issuing from "political superiors" and, in the final analysis, from the "sovereign" of a community – some person or set of persons who lays down coercive commands, enjoys habitual obedience from the bulk of the community, and is not habitually obedient to any other human being.

Austin's theory thus incorporates a very natural conception of law, as commands that are backed by sanctions. Laws are seen as brute social facts. To determine the existence of a law and what it requires or allows is to engage in an inquiry into the relevant facts: what commands have been issued by (or are otherwise attributable to) the uncommanded commanders of the community?

To determine such facts is not to judge them. Austin wrote, "The existence of law is one thing; its merit or demerit is another."[15] After one determines what the law is, one can evaluate it. That is a different inquiry altogether.

Austin's theory of law is a form of legal positivism. Legal positivists generally hold that law is a social phenomenon, and that laws are subject to appraisal from a moral point of view. In this chapter we will consider the first of those two points by examining Austin's theory and its contemporary descendant. In the next chapter we will look more closely at the relations between law and moral standards.

Law as imperative

It seems natural to think of laws as commands. In doing so, however, we have already begun to theorize about the nature of law. For laws are not usually written in the imperative mood. A criminal statute, for example, says what shall be done to a person who acts in a certain manner. In thinking of this as a command, we look beneath its superficial grammar with an understanding of how it functions. A statute is not a prediction of what will happen to a person who so behaves. Rather, it stipulates legal consequences. It is meant to be followed, to regulate the behavior of those who may be tempted so to act as well as those who are charged with administering the law – police and prosecutors, judges and juries.

It is useful to compare the imperatival conception of law with the "predictive theory" advanced by the American jurist Oliver Wendell Holmes (1841–1935). Holmes held that the study of law is concerned with "the prediction of the incidence of the public force through the instrumentality of the courts." He characterized laws as "prophecies of what courts will do in fact."[16]

Predictive theorists believe it important to emphasize the difference between "law in books" and "law in action." "Law in action" is what judges decide, while "law in books" is what one finds in academic textbooks of law and records such as statutes and judicial opinions. One reason for this difference is that judges sometimes render decisions that do not faithfully follow what has been laid down as law. Another factor – more important for the development of the predictive theory – is that "law in books" sometimes seems incapable of guiding judicial decisions, so that judges must decide cases on other grounds. Statutes can be vague or ambiguous, they can conflict with one another, and they do not always clearly cover novel cases. Furthermore, a good deal of law in the British and North American legal systems derives from judicial decisions on past cases rather than legislative enactments, and the implications of such "judicial precedents" are often controversial. Predictive theorists are concerned with the decisions actually made by judges, since these determine what *happens* to people who come before the courts. They accordingly regard the social phenomenon of law as a matter of such decisions, and predictions of such decisions as a more reliable guide to law, in this sense, than what may be written in law books.

Predictive theorists maintain that predictions provide guidelines for behavior because they tell those who are liable to come before the courts how they can expect to fare if they behave in certain ways. People wish to avoid unfavorable court decisions and will be guided accordingly. Predictive theorists understand the idea that one is required by law to behave in a certain way, as the likelihood that one who behaves differently will receive an unfavorable court decision.

The distinction between "law in books" and "law in action" is important, but the predictive theory does not seem to provide a sound analysis of law. We cannot understand a legal requirement as the likelihood of an unfavorable court decision, because it sometimes makes perfectly good sense to suppose that one who is required by law to act in a certain way is unlikely to suffer such consequences. The legal wrong may never be discovered or, if discovered, may never be brought to the attention of a court. In a similar way, we may be able to predict that someone whose behavior is legally impeccable is likely to receive an unfavorable court decision as the result of a mistake or official corruption. What the law requires or allows is one thing; what is likely to happen to people as a result of court decisions, while related, is something different.

The predictive theory seems to distort the relation of law to judicial decisions. Many of the predictions that we are able to make about court decisions *presuppose* the "law in books," for they assume that judges will follow statutes and other rules that unproblematically apply. Predictive theorists tend to ignore this because they are preoccupied with "hard cases," in which existing law is unclear or controversial. Their theory implies, in effect, that *all* cases are undecidable on the basis of existing law, for it implies that we can *never* think of judges as either following or deviating from the law. This is because predictions are not normative standards. A prediction can be confirmed or falsified by subsequent events, but it does not function as a rule, principle, or precept to be followed. If a judge's decision agrees with a prediction about how he will decide, we cannot conclude that he has decided soundly. If his decision disagrees with a prediction, we cannot infer that he has decided unsoundly. But it makes perfectly good sense to suppose that judges sometimes decide cases soundly or unsoundly, by reference to existing law. If there is any law for courts to follow, it cannot be understood in predictive terms.

The predictive theory is inadequate, then, not because there is no difference between "law in books" and "law in action," but because it employs the wrong sort of concept. Austin seems to understand this point, for it is central to his criticism of the prominent English jurist William Blackstone (1723–80).[17] Blackstone confused the idea of "law" in "laws of nature," which represent regularities in the world, with the idea of "law" as used in standards for behavior. Scientific claims about the natural order of things do not tell us how to behave, but laws do. Scientific claims are either true or false, but laws are not. In these respects, laws are like imperatives. And a plausible theory about the division of linguistic labor tells us that sentences in the declarative mood (such as predictions) purport to tell us what is (or will be) the case, while sentences in the imperative mood tell us what to do.

Law as coercive

Austin conceives of laws (or rules) as imperatival because they are meant to guide behavior. But he recognizes a difference between some action-guiding statements, such as requests or pleas, and laws. The latter impose mandatory requirements or prohibitions on behavior, whereas the former do not. The difference, Austin holds, is to be found in the fact that laws create "obligations" because they are backed by "sanctions" which are to be imposed for noncompliance. Laws are thus conceived of as essentially coercive in the sense that they are meant to motivate compliance by increasing the likelihood that those who fail to comply will suffer accordingly.

This is a plausible conception of law, which seems to be reflected in everyday thinking about it. A person often learns about law by discovering what police and courts are for and what lies ahead if one runs afoul of the law. Few legal theorists have doubted that law is coercive, and the idea has sometimes dominated jurisprudence. It underlies Bentham's remark that "a law, whatever good it may do in the long run, is sure in the first instance to produce mischief," because it threatens us with unwelcome consequences. "It may be a necessary evil," Bentham said, "but still at any rate it is an evil. To make law is to do evil that good may come."[18]

We should remember, however, that Austin's theory that laws are coercive commands is not limited to positive law, the principal subject-matter of jurisprudence, but is meant to cover all "rules" that impose "obligations." It encompasses moral principles as well as the law of a community.

Austin conceives of moral standards in this way because he believes that they are created by Divine commands. But it is possible to believe that one is under a moral obligation, that is, a genuine obligation the existence of which does not depend on social recognition or enforcement, without believing in the existence of a God. More generally, it seems to make perfectly good sense to suppose that one is under an obligation without having been commanded by anyone. I may be under an obligation to you because, for example, I have made a promise, I owe you something I have borrowed, or I have done you a wrongful injury. None of these obligations seems to presuppose that anyone has commanded anything.

One who wishes to defend a Divine command theory of moral obligation might reply that Divine commands are nevertheless the *ground* of obligations, whether or not we conceive of them in that way. So it is worth noting that some theological conceptions of morality make God's role less central than this. On the theory that seems to be required by Austin's analysis, moral standards are *whatever* God commands, *just because* God commands them. According to this theory, benevolence is morally required only because God commands us to help others. Benevolence has no merit in and of itself. One who believes this cannot accept the idea of sound moral standards without believing in a God.

But others hold that God commands us to be benevolent *because God understands* that it is morally required. On this view, Divine law reflects objective standards that are independent of God's will. If we are confident that God wills soundly, that is only because we are confident that God wishes us well. The *ground* of the obligation is thus not God's command but rather the independent moral requirement.

Austin himself suggests this way of understanding Divine law. For he believes that we can have no direct knowledge of Divine commands. We do suppose, however, that God wishes us well, and from this Austin infers that moral rules must serve the general welfare. Someone with a nonutilitarian theory of morality could accept this basic idea and modify it accordingly. The upshot is that belief in God is not required for the recognition of moral standards.

We have even less reason to accept Austin's notion that one is under an obligation only if one is liable to sanctions for noncompliance. I can believe that I am under an obligation to compensate another for a wrongful injury I have done him without supposing that I am liable to suffer sanctions for acting otherwise. One is often subject to social pressures for conformity to prevailing standards, but our ideas about morality do not limit them, as we have seen, to requirements that are generally accepted.

What about Austin's theory as it applies to positive law? The idea that laws are coercive commands seems modeled on the criminal law, which provides penalties for prohibited conduct. But this is not all there is to law even in the simplest legal systems. The criminal law itself contains a procedural part, which governs among other things the behavior of police and prosecutors, the steps to be taken before, during, and after a trial, the conduct of judges and lawyers, and the incarceration of convicted persons. While many of these regulations can be understood as restricting behavior and creating legal obligations, not all provide penalties for noncompliance. Beyond this, there are laws regulating contracts, property and exchange, currency and banking, taxation and licensing, arbitration and collective bargaining, marriage and families, social welfare programs, legislation, and many other things. Not all of these matters are regulated in any direct way by coercive commands. Can they all be comprehended by Austin's theory?

This question has been put more sharply by one of Austin's sympathetic critics, H. L. A. Hart.[19] Hart agrees that a principal function of law is to regulate behavior by restricting choices – by telling people what to do and often providing sanctions for noncompliance. This is done by what Hart calls "obligation-imposing" or "primary" rules, not only in the criminal law, which the state enforces through criminal prosecutions, but also in some branches of the "civil law," such as the law of torts, under which individuals may sue to rectify legally recognized wrongs done by others to them. The failure to comply with such a rule is, like the violation of a criminal statute, a breach of legal obligation. Although Hart rejects Austin's notion that laws – even primary rules – are coercive commands, he acknowledges that Austin's theory provides an initially plausible account of this part of the law. Hart claims, however, that other laws are not like that at all.

Consider a law which says, in effect, that someone who has reached the age of eighteen can make an agreement legally binding by signing a document stipulating the particulars and having two witnesses to the parties' signatures. This law prescribes the steps to be taken by someone who wishes a contract to be enforceable in a court of law. It does not require anyone to enter such an agreement: one is free to do so or to abstain, as one chooses. This law *facilitates* choice rather than restricting it. The failure to use or follow such a rule is not a violation of law or a breach of legal obligation, but is the failure to exercise a legal "power" conferred by the law. Hart calls such laws "power-conferring" rules and he argues that they cannot be accommodated by Austin's theory.

It is uncertain that this argument succeeds. To see this, we can be guided by Austin's own discussion of alleged counter-examples to his theory.[20] Austin does not pretend that everything ordinarily called "a law" functions like a coercive command. He believes his theory accords fairly well with linguistic usage and, most important, that it can account for every aspect of a legal system without distortion. We can understand him to say that *all the content of a body of law can accurately be represented within a set of coercive commands.*

Austin considers, for example, whether laws that create rights can be understood as coercive commands. He believes they can because he holds that laws create rights by imposing legal obligations on other persons. If legal obligations are imposed by coercive commands and every legal right corresponds to someone else's legal obligation, then Austin's answer is persuasive. What about laws that do not prohibit or restrict behavior but rather permit behavior that was previously restricted? Austin observes that such permissive laws nullify or modify existing coercive commands. They can be accommodated to his theory by noting that commands can be qualified or withdrawn. Another type of law that does not seem coercive is called "declaratory." These clarify or qualify the content of existing laws by restricting their application. No theoretical concession is required to accommodate them. Finally, Austin admits that there are also "imperfect" laws, imperatives without sanctions attached. But that, Austin says, is precisely why such incompletely formed laws are called "imperfect."

Austin's discussion suggests one way of trying to accommodate the fact that there are legal powers without surrendering the idea that laws are coercive commands which impose legal requirements. As Austin's discussion of declaratory laws implies, some things that are ordinarily called "laws" would not be counted as complete laws under his theory. But his theory might nevertheless be capable of incorporating the *content* of such incomplete laws. The example of declaratory laws suggests that coercive commands can be complex: their application may be subject to special conditions, which can be modified. Furthermore, any adequate development of Austin's theory would have to acknowledge that legal requirements are sometimes conditional. If laws are to be modeled on coercive commands, they too must be conditional. For many obligation-imposing rules are limited in scope, applying only to certain members of the community or under limited conditions. Indeed, perhaps *all* legal rules should be understood in this way, as limited in scope, because they extend no further than the acknowledged jurisdiction. British law, for example, does not generally cover conduct outside the area of British rule. An Austinian analysis of law may therefore be understood to take as the standard form of legal rule, not "Do A or else S," but rather "In condition C, do A or else S," where "A" is the description of the conduct that is required, "S" stands for the sanction, and "C" stipulates any condition that must be satisfied before the command applies in a particular case.

An Austinian might therefore try to accommodate legal powers in the following way. He would claim that what Hart calls "power-conferring" rules are not complete laws but only "fragments" of laws. Powers regulate the conditions under which people have legal obligations. An Austinian would suggest that the sample law governing contracts should be understood as saying: "If you have reached the age of eighteen and your signature on a contract has been witnessed by two other persons, then perform as it stipulates, or else S." This Austinian response acknowledges legal powers, but tries to show that they can be included in a system composed entirely of coercive commands. It does not pretend that law is exhausted by penal rules, but argues that other parts of law function in a similar manner.

But legal powers are not the only aspects of law that must be incorporated into an adequate theory. Other legal provisions are not so easily accommodated to the model of coercive commands. Consider the familar use of law to distribute benefits and services. States provide some services directly, such as education, water and sewer service, garbage disposal, and traffic regulation. They provide cash and other benefits through various programs, such as home relief, medical insurance, and aid to families with dependent children. Some of these activities are aided by restrictive rules, but it is doubtful that the entire body of social welfare law can be construed on the model of coercive commands. Many of the rules govern the behavior of public servants, and these often lack sanctions. Furthermore, the basic function of such law is not to coerce but to distribute benefits and services.

Hart makes a similar point about power-conferring rules. Even if the formal content of these laws could be contained in a complex set of coercive commands, that would distort matters because the function of such law is to facilitate choice, not restrict it. It is possible to overstate this point. Power-conferring rules can prevent children from making binding contracts, can prevent wives from holding property, and can force individuals into slavery. They can be used deliberately for such purposes. In a similar way, welfare legislation may force men and women to get married or divorced, husbands to leave the family home, and families to respect arbitrary standards if they wish to receive needed benefits or services. Nevertheless, while such law can have these effects and can even be used deliberately for these purposes, it would seem a distortion as well as an incomplete picture of social welfare legislation to focus exclusively on their restrictive aspects. For these are not essential to that sort of law.

If this is right, an Austinian might fall back to a less ambitious theoretical position. He might argue that the sort of law his theory describes is the *central* part of any legal system, without which there could be no law. He might grant that legal machinery, once established, can be used for quite different purposes. But he would claim that those aspects of the law, such as social welfare legislation, are optional rather than essential elements of a legal system.

To evaluate this claim, we must shift our focus. We have been considering whether law can be understood as a collection of coercive commands. If an Austinian holds instead that coercion is a necessary element of a legal system *as a whole*, we must ask whether there can be law without coercion *at all*. It is doubtful that we can find an example of a legal system devoid of coercive sanctions. But this does not show that there could not be a legal system without them.

To try to answer this question, we must conduct a "thought experiment." We must try to imagine a social system sufficiently like familiar legal systems so that it can accept the label "law," but which has no legally established sanctions. We need not exclude the operation of all social pressures, but no sanctions can be authorized by the law-like norms and none can be officially imposed.

Imagine that a group of individuals who are committed to constructing a utopian society have settled an isolated and independent community. They believe that punishment is costly, psychologically damaging to individuals, and poisons social life. They believe there should be no systematic enforcement of established norms. This is not to say they have no law; that remains to be seen. We can imagine that they create forms of social organization that are (so far as possible) otherwise identical to the rule of law. We can imagine that they meet to determine the basic ground rules for their community and establish procedures for legislating regular rules of behavior, exchange, and adjudication to deal with disputes and rule violations. They can select some of their members to occupy official positions. The only thing we cannot let them do is provide for sanctions or any system of enforcement.

However the details of such a system should be worked out, it would clearly have no hope of success unless its members were unusually committed to reaching agreement and capable of adhering to it. This may show that such an idea cannot be realized in practice. But it would not show that the idea does not make sense, for while the required commitment and determination may be rare, it is not humanly impossible. We may therefore be able to populate our imaginary community with suitable individuals. If we then construct the example carefully, we may find no good reason to deny that these people have a legal system, though it is devoid of legal sanctions. If that is possible, then sanctions may be practically indispensable, given people as they are, but they are not built into the very concept of law. Sanctions may be a price we have to pay for ordinary human conflict, competition, selfishness, and frailty.

Given the world as it is, sanctions may not just limit liberty but also enhance it. One's legal liberty might be measured by the absence of coercive restrictions on behavior, but the effective exercise of liberty and enjoyment of it requires that others' interference be securely limited. If others are likely to interfere unless they are restrained, then coercive regulations may not only provide social stability but also make whatever legal liberty we have more valuable. Considerations like these suggest the practical value of coercive law. But they do not support the minimal Austinian idea that coercion is part of the very concept of law.

The Austinian sovereign

Austin believes that any coercive command is a law "properly so called." Divine commands impose such laws. Coercive commands are issued by individuals acting outside the law. Positive law must therefore be distinguished from other rules, both human and Divine.

What distinguishes positive law in Austin's theory is its peculiar source – the "sovereign" of a community, some determinate person or set of persons whose coercive commands are habitually obeyed by the bulk of the community and who are not habitually obedient to anyone else. Everything that counts as positive law must be attributable to the sovereign, and nothing else counts as positive law.[21]

The idea of a sovereign serves other theoretical purposes. It helps Austin explain the independence of one legal system from others. It also helps to explain how some things that are not coercive commands, such as declaratory and imperfect laws, are part of the legal system: they all issue from the sovereign.

Austin's use of the term "sovereign" does not mean that he assumes all legal systems are like absolute monarchies. Austin believes that any legal system, however democratic, must be understood to have some ultimate law makers. This notion – or something like it – is not an optional aspect of his theory. Nor is it required chiefly for the purpose of distinguishing positive law from other standards. The inner logic of his analysis of laws as coercive commands leads inexorably to some such theoretical notion.

Austin recognizes that laws in the sense relevant to his inquiry set standards for behavior and must be distinguished from laws of nature. This leads him to the idea that laws are imperatives. But the imperatives in law must be distinguished from requests and entreaties: they set requirements on conduct. This leads him to the idea that laws are coercive imperatives or commands. But commands issue from commanders, and the model of commands leads to the idea that laws issue from a distinctive sort of commander – the Austinian sovereign.

It is clear that a theory like Austin's must be developed further to account for the complexity of legal organization. Perhaps we can conceive of a system along the lines suggested by the Austinian idea of a "sovereign," with one or a few individuals making all the rules. But most legal systems are more complex than that. They contain a hierarchy of officials and a division of official labor. Some officials are subordinate to others. Some make law, others enforce it. Some try cases, others review them on appeal.

The complex internal organization of legal systems is at least in part a matter of law. Law does not simply issue from legislative bodies but also creates those bodies, regulates appointments to them, and establishes procedures within them. Courts are established and their powers determined by law. The same holds for the "executive" branch of government: these official positions are established by law.

For the Austinian theory to provide an adequate analysis of law, all of this law must be reducible to a complex set of coercive commands. Most important, it must be possible to account for all of this law by attributing it to an Austinian sovereign.

That seems to be impossible. If we apply the Austinian theory, we quickly find that some law, such as that found in written constitutions, is not regarded as legally binding because it issues from some specific individuals who currently rule, that is, individuals who are identified by the fact that they issue coercive commands that are generally obeyed and who are not generally obedient to any other human beings. Even when we can trace laws, such as recent legislation, to those who currently rule, we do not identify those rulers in that way, but rather by the fact that they occupy official positions. Furthermore, they hold such offices and the offices are established according to law. And this law – the law that confers legal authority on specific individuals – cannot be accounted for by tracing it, in turn, to those individuals themselves. This law is *presupposed* by their status as officials. Austin has the cart before the horse.

The same basic problem reappears in different forms when we try to apply Austin's theory to various aspects of a legal system or types of legal organization. Austin believes, for example, that his theory can accommodate the idea of "popular sovereignty."[22] He suggests that in such a system the entire electorate must be counted as the sovereign. But we cannot identify the members of the electorate without having recourse to those legal rules that establish voting privileges. In such a system we also find in extreme form a paradox of the Austinian theory: the commanders must be understood to command themselves. The Austinian theory of sovereignty is based on the notion that the very concept of law implies a coercive power relation within a community: some make rules that others are expected to obey and those who make the rules impose their will by means of threats. This model most clearly breaks down in the case of popular sovereignty, for then all must be understood as having such a relation to themselves, which is nonsense. But the problem is not limited to such a system, because it is commonplace for law makers to be subject to laws of their own making. The point is not that this cannot happen, but that Austin's theory cannot contemplate the possibility. We can make rules that apply to ourselves – but not by issuing coercive commands to ourselves. The model of coercive commands will not work.

These objections might seem politically naive. They might

appear to ignore the way in which law is sometimes trampled by those who acquire power. But the idea of trampling law assumes its existence. The argument is not that law conferring legal authority is always respected, but that it is presupposed by any claims about legal authority. If a community lacks any provision for assignments of authority, conditions central to a legal system would seem to be absent.

Austin's theory may seem appealing because it places great emphasis on the role of coercive power relations within a political community. But the objections to Austin's theory do not deny that coercion may be needed to maintain a system of law or that law may be violated by those who acquire power. They draw attention to the failure of a particular attempt to understand these phenomena.

The idea of authority is at the heart of a legal system. Individuals are authorized to make decisions in the name of the law by virtue of occupying established offices and following prescribed procedures. Legal requirements are identified not by tracing them to specific individuals but by legal tests. Our task now is to understand this better.

Law as the union of primary and secondary rules

H. L. A. Hart's theory of law, currently the most widely accepted theory, is built on lessons drawn from systematic criticism of Austin's analysis. In *The Concept of Law*, Hart points out three principal defects in Austin's theory which he seeks to rectify.[23] First, Hart believes that Austin's model of coercive commands is not adequate to explain "primary" rules, which impose obligations. Second, Hart claims that law includes rules which confer powers and which cannot be reduced to rules imposing obligations. Third, Hart argues that the foundation of a legal system is a collection of "secondary" rules which regulate the creation of law, its application, and, most important, its authoritative identification.

Hart, like Austin, regards law as a matter of rules. The existence of a rule is a species of social fact. In this respect, Hart does not deviate from Austin's general approach to legal theory. But his analysis of rules is different.

Hart distinguishes two conditions under which rules may be said to exist. The first is social acceptance. When a number of individuals regard a standard as appropriate – when they internalize that standard – the corresponding rule exists. They regard some pattern of behavior as required and deviations from that standard as lapses subject to legitimate criticism. When such a standard is backed by strong social pressures for conformity, it is regarded as imposing obligations. When the obligation is considered especially important and falls within the capacity of individuals to perform, it is considered moral. This accounts for most of what Austin calls positive morality. Hart, however, treats this as a theory of moral obligation. He maintains, in effect, that moral obligations are determined by socially accepted rules.[24]

Although socially accepted rules have only limited importance within Hart's theory of law, some comments on his general theory of obligation are in order. Hart seems right in holding that one who accepts a moral standard as imposing an obligation is committed to certain other normative notions, such as that a deviation is a lapse subject to criticism. The idea that one is under an obligation is essentially connected not with coercion or commands but with moral appraisal of the relevant conduct. Hart, however, seems to be wrong in suggesting that a moral obligation exists when and only when there is social acceptance of the appropriate standard. For, just as it makes good sense to suppose that one is under an obligation in the absence of commands or sanctions, it makes good sense to suppose both that one can be under an obligation which is not generally recognized and that one may not be under an obligation even though everyone else believes one is. Hart's theory of obligation commits him to an implausible form of moral conventionalism.

In any case, legal rules do not generally exist because of social acceptance. Law can contain unpopular provisions, the legal status of which is not controversial, and the authoritative determination of what is law does not typically include a test of popular support. Hart accordingly recognizes a second condition under which a rule may be said to exist. It might satisfy tests laid down within a complex institution such as the law. One type of test is provided by the rules regulating legislation: laws can be enacted by legislative bodies following prescribed procedures. There are other tests for law used in legal systems. Judicial precedents may be counted as establishing law. Customary practices may be a source of law. What counts as law, Hart claims, depends on the regular practice of officials who are authorized to determine what counts as law. The criteria that they use may be explicitly laid down in other law, such as written constitutions, or may have become entrenched in law over time by the regular practice of the courts. The criteria that officials use to identify what counts as law within a particular system can be thought of as collected in what Hart calls "rules of recognition." Each system can be thought of as having a basic rule of recognition which corresponds to the most fundamental criteria regularly used by its officials to decide what counts as law. In the British system, for example, the basic rule of recognition may be stated (somewhat misleadingly) as the rule that whatever the Queen in Parliament enacts is law. In the United States essential reference must be made to its written constitution and, within each of the several states, to its own distinct state constitution.

Hart's theory seeks to reconcile two diverse aspects of a legal system: it is regulated by law which is shaped by the practice of officials. What counts as law depends on other law, but the law on which it ultimately depends – the basic rule of recognition – amounts to the tests that officials accept and use. Most legal rules exist because they meet the legal tests and are considered "legally valid." But this, Hart holds, cannot be true of the basic rule of recognition itself. It *provides* the tests for law and is not tested in a similar way. The basic rule of recognition is a function of officials' shared attitudes and practices and is therefore a matter of social acceptance within that limited subcommunity of officials. According to Hart, law is a "union of primary and secondary rules" which are generally observed within a community. It is necessary to include the point of general observance in order to distinguish an actually functioning legal system from one that has been replaced or that might be proposed.

According to Hart, therefore, law is a species of social fact. The sort of fact involved is highly complex, for it includes (i) acceptance of the rule of recognition by officials, (ii) the implications of the rule of recognition (whether putative laws satisfy those tests), and (iii) general conformity by the community to the valid laws.

Hart's theory provides us with a sketch of a complex social phenomenon. One of his objectives is to distinguish law from other social phenomena. This aim is partly achieved by his distinction between social acceptance and validity as conditions for the existence of rules. But it is unclear that the larger task of distinguishing law from other social phenomena is achieved.

Many organizations have a structure that is identical to a legal system as Hart describes it. A club or voluntary organization has basic rules, rules that satisfy tests for validity employed within the organization, official positions that are regulated by valid rules, primary rules that regulate the behavior of the membership, and a membership that generally observes the applicable rules. What distinguishes any such organization from law?

Hart does not address this question. If no answer can be constructed out of the materials he provides or by supplementing his theory, then something has gone wrong. We wish to know not only how law resembles other aspects of social life but also what is distinctive about it.

The question that we face is this: can we think of any essential aspects of a legal system that are not explicitly identified by Hart's analysis but serve to distinguish law from analogous social phenomena? Some possible candidates come quickly to mind. An examination of them will suggest the difficulty that we face.

It might be held that law, unlike other social institutions, is essentially coercive. We have considered this idea, however, and made the following suggestion: it seems possible to conceive of a system much like law but lacking authoritative sanctions. Given typical conditions, such a system may be impractical, but it does not follow that sanctions are an essential feature of law. More important, social organizations of various kinds have sanctions of their own. If so, law's typical use of sanctions cannot differentiate law from institutions with similar internal structures.

It is nevertheless commonly said that the law – or alternatively the political state – enjoys a "monopoly" on the use of force within a community. If other institutions employ sanctions, how is this to be understood? It must mean that from the standpoint of the law sanctions may be used only with its permission. For present purposes, however, this proves nothing, since that is not necessarily the way those other institutions view their own use of sanctions from their own perspectives. A church, for example, may well regard the law's use of sanctions as illegitimate unless that use can be justified on principles that the church itself accepts. If so, the church's attitude towards sanctions is analogous to that of the law, and this aspect of law could not be cited as a distinguishing feature of the law.

It might be held that law enjoys a uniquely authoritative status relative to other institutions within a community. Many social organizations, for example, may be said to exist only at the pleasure of the law. This is certainly true in some cases, such as commercial corporations, which are creatures of economic arrangements established by law. Once again, however, there are difficulties with this way of differentiating law from other social institutions. In the first place, not all social institutions are creatures of the law in the way that corporations are. People can join together to form associations with complex internal structures, analogous to that found in the law, without having recourse to legal rules, without relying on legal enforcement of their private arrangements. In the second place, this way of looking at the relative status of the law is framed in legal terms. If we look at the relations between the law and other institutions from the perspectives of those other organizations, we will find that they too can have values or norms by which to measure their own relations with the law and that the law is not then always regarded as enjoying superior status or authority. Take once more the example of a church. Just as the law may regard a church's activities as lawful or unlawful, so the church may regard the law's activities as religious or irreligious, moral or immoral, and as meriting no more respect than law can earn by functioning well, according to the church's standards. The law appears supreme within a community only if we look at such relations from the law's perspective. But if another institution can regard itself, from its perspective, as having more legitimate authority than law, this aspect of the law cannot distinguish law from other institutions generally.

It might be held that law, unlike the norms of other social institutions, governs the entire community. This cannot be taken to mean, of course, that the entire community respects the law, since that is not always the case, but only that the law's authority is conceived of as extending throughout the political community. Difficulties face this suggestion too. First, nothing prevents another institution from regarding its norms as applicable to all members of a given community. Second, the relevant community is defined at least in part by the organization in question. The law defines the relevant political community; a church, for example, defines the community of those whom it regards as subject to its legitimate authority. Nor is a church the only institution of which this may be true. Any institution that regards itself as having legitimate authority to set norms for people to follow, even if they do not voluntarily join the social grouping, is analogous to the law in this respect.

The difficulties we have found with these ways of supplementing Hart's theory of law, in order to com-plete it, suggest that something may be fundamentally wrong with the present approach. Two possibilities may be mentioned.

The first possibility is suggested by the very idea that law is a matter of social fact, amenable to empirical study. There may be limits to analytic jurisprudence which concern its relations to empirical studies, such as legal anthropology.

Traditional jurisprudence assumes, in effect, that what counts as law is to be determined by conceptual analysis – a careful explication of the idea of law, or rather the particular idea that is associated with the idea of a legal system, which draws appropriate distinctions between this idea of law and closely related ideas with which it might be confused. Philosophers of law sometimes seem to assume that the results of such conceptual analysis determine the proper boundaries of associated empirical studies. The anthropology of law, for example, may be conceived as having a subject-matter that is determined by the conceptual analysis of law.

As it happens, social scientists do not approach their studies in this way, and this does not seem to be merely a matter of disciplinary insularity. Legal phenomena are identified not so much by reference to the familiar features of legal systems, such as courts and legislative authorities, but rather in terms of certain social functions, such as dispute resolution and the social control of behavior. These social functions are performed by a variety of social arrangements outside as well as inside legal systems, even when legal systems exist. One who is trained in traditional jurisprudence might be tempted to regard such an approach as muddled, confusing legal phenomena ("properly so called," as Austin might put it) with other social phenomena from which they should be distinguished. But that reaction might be misguided. To see this, we must consider how our ideas about the world are affected by empirical studies in other spheres.

Throughout developed science, one finds that our prescientific ideas serve as only first approximations of the way the world is really organized. They are liable to be modified or displaced by conceptions that depend on the successful development of scientific theory. Our prescientific idea of water, for example, referred to readily identifiable properties of substances. Water was conceived of as a tasteless, colorless liquid (or something of that sort). But the development of physical theory has shown this to be, literally, crude and superficial, in the sense that it does not satisfactorily correspond to the underlying physical reality. Physical science enables us to understand that the same substance can exist in different states, because it identifies that substance in relation to significant regularities in nature which are rooted in microscopic structures and relations. As a consequence, some of the things we might originally have classified as water are now understood to be composed of other substances, and some of the things that we might originally not have classified with water we can now understand to be identical with it in physically important respects.

If we conceive of the world as having no natural "joints" – as a collection of phenomena which are unregulated by natural law – then any arbitrary set of concepts, any manner of drawing distinctions, might be adequate for describing it. A set of concepts would simply serve as a way of systematizing thought about the world. But even to suppose that one way of thinking about the world has some practical advantages over other possible schemes is to suppose that there are causal regularities among natural phenomena, knowledge of which we can use in making things happen. And there is no reason to assume that natural laws are excluded from the social realm. Quite the contrary.

So, if we think of legal phenomena as amenable to empirical study, then we must entertain the possibility that increased understanding of the social realities which underlie legal phenomena will affect our very idea of what counts as law. The concept of law that we currently have may provide us with no more than a first approximation of the natural "joints" within the social world.

There are of course important differences between legal phenomena and the subject-matter of physical science, the most important of which seems to be the following. Much of social reality is not merely "given" by nature but is a product of human activity and is *shaped* by human ideas. Like other social phenomena, legal phenomena *presuppose ideas* in ways that physical phenomena do not.

Furthermore, some of the relevant ideas vary: they are "relative to culture." This complicates enormously the study of legal phenomena. Thus, our idea of individual accountability for our acts and their consequences is not a cultural invariant. An ethic of guilt is different from an ethic of shame. Any study of legal phenomena must take variations like these into account.

It does not follow, however, that social reality is not regulated in significant ways by natural laws of cause and effect. Societies are organized in a variety of ways, but always within constraints of human psychology, social dynamics, and economic relations, which themselves are subjects for systematic study. How much of social reality is culturally variable and how much is invariant because of underlying natural laws remains to be seen. But we have good reason to believe that there is much to be discovered by scientific study of social reality.

We have no reason to assume that analytic studies of law have reached their limits. But an understanding of the relations between law and other social institutions may depend on the successful development of social theory. What distinguishes what we ordinarily call law from other social institutions, as well as what is common to them, and how important these similarities and differences really are is something that we cannot assume is discoverable merely by careful explication of our current concepts.

A different possibility is suggested by those who view the law in moral terms. We have already seen that one of the important elements of law, obscured by Austin's theory, is the idea of authority. A closely related notion is legitimacy. Terms like these suggest that law is not morally neutral. That might help to explain what is distinctive about the law. If it were true, in any case, it would be an important fact about the law, relevant not just to theory but also to practice.

That is the problem to which we now turn.

3

Morality in law

Is law just a matter of social fact? Or does it have some essential contact with morality? In this chapter we shall consider ways in which law may be thought to have a moral dimension.

There seems little doubt that law interacts with moral opinions. Laws governing sexual conduct, the use of narcotic substances, property, contracts, and a host of other matters have been motivated, to some degree at least, by ideas about moral rights and responsibilities. Law is shaped by the values that people have – the values of those who are able to affect the development of law. The law also has an impact on moral attitudes; its enforcement, for example, tends to reinforce the values it reflects.

Some of the connections between law and moral ideas may be systematic. All systems of social organization seem to have some prohibitions on the use of force against individuals. It has been argued that social systems cannot survive unless they incorporate some protections for persons, property, and promises.[25] But these restrictions are quite variable, and some favored groups within a society may enjoy protections that are not enjoyed by all. So, while law may reflect prevailing moral opinion, its restrictions do not necessarily correspond to sound moral principles.

But it may be possible for sound moral standards (if there are any) to become part of the law. The Fifth Amendment to the United States Constitution says that "No person shall be ...

deprived of life, liberty, or property, without due process of law." According to one interpretation,[26] this means that no one may be deprived of life, liberty, or property except as the result of a *fair* legal procedure. On this reading, the Due Process Clause assumes that we can distinguish between fair and unfair procedures. Given the doctrine of judicial review, this means that courts cannot correctly apply the Due Process Clause without exercising sound moral judgment concerning the fairness of procedures. As valid law depends on its satisfying sound moral tests, law is made to depend (so far as that is possible) on moral truth.

The last example is more closely related to our present concerns than those previously mentioned. This is because it claims there are connections between law and moral truth, not just between law and moral opinions. Law must meet sound moral tests. But even this example does not suggest that there are connections between law and morality of the sort that legal theorists have debated. In all of the examples given, the connections between law and morality are matters of contingent fact. The Due Process Clause, for example, is not an unavoidable feature of a legal system, and the clause could be removed from the US Constitution. The connections that legal theorists have debated are "necessary," not contingent. They are thought by some to flow from the very nature of law.

The idea that law and morality are *essentially* connected is expressed by the claim that "an unjust law is no law at all." This claim is associated with traditional ideas of "natural law," and we have seen how it is suggested by Aquinas. The claim appears paradoxical, for it seems to say that something which *is* law (unjust law) is *not* law. But that is misleading. It may be like the claim that a counterfeit dollar is not a real dollar: an unjust law is so much a perversion of the idea of law that it cannot be counted as a law at all. That would dissolve the paradox.

But can the claim be true? It seems difficult to deny that laws can intelligibly be judged good or bad, wise or foolish, just or unjust. If there *are* moral standards by which laws may properly be judged, then it would seem that laws can *be* good or bad, just or unjust. And, as we have seen, Aquinas's apparent endorsement of this traditional natural law claim is itself misleading, since he agrees that laws framed by humans are either just or unjust.

This suggests that, if there are essential connections between law and morality, they must be more subtle and less obvious. That is the possibility we must explore. But first we must see how this possibility is compatible with the seemingly undeniable fact that law is a social phenomenon.

The separation of law and morals

Much of legal theory has centered on disputes between "natural lawyers" and "legal positivists" who disagree about the relations between morality and law. Positivists embrace "the separation of law and morals" whereas natural lawyers are said to deny it. Our discussion of moral judgment will help us understand what is at stake.

When Austin says, "The existence of law is one thing; its merit or demerit is another," he is understood as endorsing the positivistic view. But what, exactly, is he saying? And why does he say it?

One thing he seems to mean is that law is not necessarily good, right, and just. Law does not necessarily satisfy the standards by which it may properly be judged. Law is morally fallible.

But Austin appears to be saying more than this, and another thing that he might mean is suggested by the social conception of law. Positive law is rooted in human history and institutions. It is shaped by human actions and decisions and is subject to control by human beings. To determine what the law is we must engage in an empirical inquiry about the relevant facts. By contrast, to determine whether law is good or bad, just or unjust, we must evaluate it. That is another inquiry altogether.

This suggests a line of argument that may be attributed to the jurist Hans Kelsen (1881–1973).[27] Social facts determine what laws exist and what they require and allow. These are a matter of objective fact. But moral judgments have no basis in fact; they simply express the attitudes that we have. So it is impossible for law to be a function of morality. The identification and interpretation of law must be independent of moral conditions.

This line of reasoning might explain why some have accepted the separation of law and morals and based it on a social conception of law. But it seems to prove too much. If moral judgments were totally subjective, as Kelsen seems to have held, then it would make little sense to suggest, as Austin does, that law *has* "merit" or "demerit." One might judge law, but there would be no standards by which law could properly be judged. The idea that law is morally fallible would be, at best, misleading.

Kelsen's reasoning assumes some form of moral skepticism. This is not the view endorsed by most legal positivists. Bentham, Austin, and many contemporary positivists believe that moral judgments are not inherently arbitrary. They might distinguish between the sort of empirical inquiry that identifies and interprets law and the sort of inquiry that is required for its evaluation, but they would not disparage evaluations.

One might nevertheless suppose that the social conception of law – the idea that law is a matter of social fact – commits one to the separation of law and morals, or at least to the notion that law is morally fallible. For human beings and their conduct are morally fallible, so it may seem natural to infer that law, which is shaped by human beings and is subject to their control, is morally fallible too. But this is not a valid argument.

According to the social conception of law, the existence and content of law are determined by some range of social facts. The social conception tells us only that much; it does not tell us *which* specific facts are relevant. That is the task of a specific theory of law, such as Austin's or Hart's. We do not yet have a well-confirmed social theory of law, so we do not know what social facts are fundamentally relevant.

Let us suppose, however, for the sake of argument, that a

social theory of law could be established. It would tell us what social facts are relevant to determining law. Let us refer to these facts, whatever they might be, as *law-determining* facts. To suppose that the social conception of law entails that law is morally fallible is to suppose that law-determining facts do *not* insure that law has positive moral value. But this inference would be invalid. The conclusion may be true, but the social conception of law does not require it.

If ethical nihilism is not assumed, we must allow that some form of "ethical naturalism" may be correct. Moral value may itself be determined by some range of facts. Utilitarians believe that moral value is determined by the promotion of welfare; social relativists believe that moral value is determined by consensus. Possibilities like these cannot be ignored, and they are not excluded by the social conception of law. For all the social conception of law tells us, it is possible that law-determining facts include the very facts that confer positive moral value on law.

In order to argue from the social conception of law to the moral fallibility of law, we would need to show that law-determining facts do not insure that law has positive moral value. It is difficult to see how this could be done without providing both a well-confirmed social theory of law, which specifies the facts that are relevant to the existence and content of law (a theory we do not yet have), and a well-confirmed moral theory (which we also do not have). We would need to know not just what facts determine law but also what facts, if any, determine moral value. The social conception of law – the general claim that law is a matter of objective social facts – does not provide this.

The possibility that law-determining facts might insure that law *has* positive moral value must be taken seriously, not just for general theoretical reasons but also because a claim of this type is endorsed by many legal writers. Suppose that a court must decide a novel case concerning one person's responsibility for another's loss. The court rules that A must pay damages to B because A did an act of type X in circumstances C. Let us suppose, further, that this judgment has the force of legal precedent and so becomes a rule of law. Within that court's jurisdiction, the next time someone sues another to compensate a loss resulting from the latter's doing an act of type X in circumstances C, the court must rule in a similar way. (This assumes that the second case cannot be "distinguished" from the first because of some relevant differences between them.) Facts like these *determine* the law governing the second case. Now, many who have written about the law believe that justice requires us to "treat like cases alike." They believe, further, that justice in the application of the law to particular cases requires that cases be considered alike or different on the basis of existing law. They believe, in other words, that justice in the application of the law requires following its general rules, so far as that is possible. They accordingly believe that justice requires treating the second case just like the first. But this amounts to holding that the relevant law-determining facts insure that a sound judicial decision in the second case will have positive moral value: this application of the law will be just if, and only if, the law is followed.

This shows that law-determining facts are sometimes thought to include facts that confer positive moral value on some aspect of the law. The social conception of law does not exclude this possibility.

So the social conception of law does not entail that law is morally fallible. But the same holds for any specific social theory of law, such as Austin's or Hart's. Such a theory only claims to tell us which facts are legally relevant. It says nothing at all about what facts, if any, are morally relevant.

What, then, is the relation between the social conception of law and the idea that law is morally fallible? There is no doubt in anyone's mind that law is morally fallible. But this conclusion does not depend on legal theory. It reflects our use of moral judgment. We can identify some norms as law and we judge that some are morally deficient. We may not be able to establish, at the theoretical level, that law is morally fallible, but we are sometimes able to judge that laws are bad, wrong, or unjust, and this tells us that law is morally fallible.

The doctrine that law is morally fallible is not a finding of legal theory but a regulating principle. We must assume – at least as a working hypothesis – that any sound legal theory must leave room for moral criticism of law. Any theory implying that law is inherently good, right, and just will bear a heavy burden of implausibility.

We should consider in the light of this discussion the suggestion sometimes made that the study of law should be "value-free." What may be meant is that, since law is a matter of social fact, the "science of law," like any social science, should investigate those facts without the intrusion of moral judgment. Such advice may be useful in some contexts, as we have seen, but it would not be helpful to us here. We have no well-confirmed social theory of law, so we cannot assume that law is *simply* a matter of social fact. We cannot assume that law has no significant connections with morality, since that is the question that we seek to answer. And we cannot entertain possible relations between law and morality without the help of moral judgment or theory. We cannot decide whether there are significant connections between law and morality unless we are prepared to identify values by which law can properly be judged.

The claim that law is morally fallible is "weak": it does not say much. If it is based on examples of immoral laws, it means only that *not all* laws automatically satisfy moral standards. It cannot mean that there are no moral constraints on what counts as law. For all such examples tell us it is possible that every legal system must embody and respect *some* moral standards. If this were the case, some parts of the law would be morally fallible but other parts would not.

We can construct a stronger version of the claim that law is morally fallible. This would insist that there are no moral constraints on what can count as law. Any moral constraints on law are contingent; none are necessary. They are determined by the law of a particular system and not by the very nature of law.

Disagreement about this might be the basis for the conflict between natural law and legal positivism. For the dispute cannot be understood in terms of the weaker claim that law is morally fallible. That is because natural lawyers do not generally maintain that law is morally infallible. We have already seen that one of the great figures of the natural law tradition, Thomas Aquinas, acknowledged the moral fallibility of human law. The same holds for many other (if not all) natural lawyers. So we might suppose that natural lawyers and legal positivists disagree about the stronger thesis, natural lawyers claiming that there are necessarily some moral constraints on what can count as law, legal positivists denying this.

The two traditions are, however, too unclear for us to be certain that this is the best way of understanding what they disagree about. Sometimes legal positivists appear to believe that natural lawyers regard law as morally infallible. This misunderstanding confuses the dispute between the two traditions. Partisans on both sides often seem to be talking at cross-purposes. We can pursue the general issues, however, without defining their dispute or worrying about the proper definition of either "natural law" or "legal positivism."

Legal and moral obligation

The law is filled with talk of rights and duties, obligation and responsibility, justice and justification. Terms that have a natural home within morality pervade the law. Is this an accident of language, a reflection of the common origins of moral and legal ideas? Or does it represent a deep-seated facet of the law?

Holmes believed that legal rhetoric is misleading. "If you want to know the law and nothing else," he said, "you must look at it as a bad man, who cares only for the material consequences which such knowledge enables him to predict." When studying law, one should wash notions like duty "with cynical acid."[28] Holmes said this, not because he wished judges to be amoral and did not care whether law was good or bad, but because he believed that our responsibilities as citizens, lawyers, and public officials are disserved when we read moral values into the law. Sometimes law is good, sometimes it is bad, and we do mischief by assuming otherwise. A lawyer advising a client, for example, must be careful not to read the law in moral terms. If he assumes that morally justifiable conduct is not subject to legal sanctions, he may counsel his client badly, and his client will suffer the consequences.

This attitude is widely shared. Bentham and Austin, for example, devoted much attention to the analysis of basic legal concepts because they held that law could not be criticized intelligently unless its fundamental features were first identified and understood. Like Holmes, they were concerned to dispel moralistic confusions about the law because they wished us to see the law for what it is and to direct it in morally more justifiable ways. We must separate moral and legal issues because law is not inherently dedicated to the interests that it ought to serve.

Holmes may be right: the use of a common vocabulary by law and morals may be misleading. That is a phenomenon that we might need to explain away. When we come to understand the way the world is ordered, we sometimes find it necessary to explain away appearances. We learn, for example, why an iron rod suddenly looks bent when immersed part way in water. That appearance does not correspond to reality, and it can be explained away by a highly confirmed theory of optics. We can then be satisfied that the rod is not really bent, visual appearances notwithstanding. That law's sharing a vocabulary with morality is similarly misleading is a possibility we should not ignore. Their common vocabulary seems to clash with the immoral purposes for which law is sometimes used and the unconscionable treatment some receive at its hands.

We may be able to explain why law misleadingly uses language like that of morality, and not just on historical grounds. Those in power have clear reason to wrap their rule in moral terms. Furthermore, the psychological mechanisms at work go well beyond deliberate attempts to gain popular support or confuse political issues. They can include powerful drives toward self-deception. Who wishes, after all, to think of himself as an instrument of injustice? Officials bound to the law and lawyers who accept their places within the system may find it agreeable to couch their discussion of legal issues in moral terminology, as if to imply that courts are doing justice when they really serve to reinforce social inequity. This would not be just a pretence but a way to maintain one's self-respect.

But we cannot assume this at the outset. Let us look more closely at the shared vocabulary of law and morality.

Those who seek to analyze basic legal concepts often concentrate on the idea of duty or obligation. This is presumably because, whatever else law is capable of doing, it creates restrictions on behavior – requirements and prohibitions that determine what conduct is minimally acceptable within the system. The same seems true within morality. We judge motives, character, laws, and many other things in moral terms, and we do not limit our appraisals by considering only what is minimally acceptable from a moral standpoint, but recognize moral achievement beyond rock-bottom moral requirements. But moral systems seem always to contain some conception of what is required and prohibited, which are usually thought of in terms of duty or obligation.

The requirements of law and morality are not equivalent, and the differences do not turn entirely on the fallibility of law. Moral standards are often more extensive and more demanding than those established by law. Morality may require generosity and compassion, charity and mercy, that fall beyond the reach of legal requirements. Despite this, the idea of a moral requirement seems analogous to that of a legal requirement.

Although "duty" and "obligation" are sometimes used in special, limited ways, so that not every requirement of law or morality would most naturally be described by using these terms, usage is somewhat loose. It will simplify our discussion to follow tradition and discuss the possible analogies in terms of duty and obligation. Distinctions important in other contexts will not affect the parallels we shall consider.

Many writers treat legal and moral obligation as two species of a single genus. Austin's theory develops the analogy in terms of coercive commands. On his view, an obligation exists when, but only when, behavioral guidelines are backed by sanctions. We have found that theory to be deficient. Legal requirements do not depend on coercive commands, and the idea seems even less suited to morality. But these defects of his theory do not entitle us to infer that moral and legal obligation are not analogous.

A central defect in Austin's theory is its neglect of what may be called the "normative" aspects of concepts like obligation. As Hart expressed the point, one who asserts the existence of an obligation implies that he accepts a standard of appraisal. To believe an obligation exists is to think that contrary conduct is a lapse or fault which is subject to sound criticism.

According to Hart, this is part of the very idea of obligation. For that reason, Hart's theory implies that sound criticism of behavior can be grounded on the existence of either legal or moral standards. One may be held at fault for failing to live up to a legal obligation just as one may be held at fault in the moral case. The conditions under which the two kinds of standard may be said to exist are different, and the two sets of requirements are not coextensive. The two kinds of obligation and the two modes of criticism are accordingly given different labels.

Hart's theory implies that if I break the law, my conduct is subject to sound criticism; likewise, if I act immorally, my conduct is subject to sound criticism. Valid criticism of behavior might be based on either law or morality – one without the other – or may be based on both sorts of requirements. If I violate one sort of requirement, there is one ground for criticism of my conduct. If I violate both at the same time, because my conduct fails to satisfy the minimal requirements of both law and morality, then there are two distinct grounds for criticism of my conduct. This might be understood in the following way: when I violate both legal and moral requirements at the same time, my conduct is doubly deficient, in the way that it would be doubly deficient were I to lie and break a promise at the same time. On this view, my conduct is *worse* than it would have been had I violated only one requirement.

In other words, we might think of legal and moral requirements as coordinate bases for evaluating conduct, so that a defect of one type can be compounded by a defect of the other type. Legal and moral obligations would then be understood as valid grounds for criticism in a common currency.

This is what Hart seems to suggest. That is because Hart conceives of obligation simply as a function of established rules. Some of the relevant rules are legal, and exist because they are "valid," while others are moral, and exist because they are generally accepted. Both sorts of rules support criticisms of conduct. Moreover, although Hart acknowledges that legally valid and socially accepted rules may themselves be subjected to criticism, he does not take this to undermine the requirements that they determine.

This picture is, I think, misleading and the difficulty stems from a mistaken analysis of moral obligation. The reason why Hart finds that moral and legal obligation are coordinate grounds for the appraisal of conduct is that he conceives of moral obligation as purely conventional. According to Hart's theory, if it is generally agreed within a community that a wife must defer to the wishes of her husband – if it is generally agreed that this is her obligation, so that her insisting on an equal voice in matters of mutual concern would be regarded as a lapse or fault subject to criticism – then a wife *is* under that obligation. Suppose, however, that someone denies the existence of such an obligation while acknowledging the social consensus to the contrary. On Hart's view, that person is not only morally mistaken, he is conceptually confused; he has not mastered this corner of our common language. But that is implausible. No one reasons about obligations in that way. It makes perfectly good sense to suppose that one lacks an obligation which others believe one has, and it makes perfectly good sense to suppose that one is under an obligation which others do not recognize. Specific moral beliefs like these might be mistaken, but they are not conceptually confused.

We can agree with Hart about the general normative implications of moral obligation. To believe that one is under an obligation is to think there is a corresponding standard for conduct, breach of which is a lapse or fault subject to sound criticism. If that is part of the very idea of obligation, then if one *is* actually under an obligation, there *is* in fact a corresponding standard which provides a valid basis for the appraisal of conduct. Whether a wife's failure to defer to the wishes of her husband constitutes a lapse or fault depends on whether she is actually under such an obligation. If she is not, then her so behaving provides no sound basis for criticism of her behavior.

Hart is right in thinking that moral obligation is linked with the conditions for immoral behavior and the grounds for moral criticism, but he is wrong in thinking these are determined by a social consensus. Legal obligation is another matter. Law is not a matter of consensus, but it does appear to be essentially conventional in other ways.

If legal requirements impose obligations but law is morally fallible, then legal requirements can be unjustified. If so, then legal obligations provide a ground for criticism of behavior only in a qualified sense. The breach of a legal obligation constitutes a lapse or fault in the eyes of the law, but not necessarily in any other respect.

This suggests a significant difference between legal and moral obligation. To take claims about moral obligations seriously, we must assume that ethical nihilism is mistaken. If so, then sound moral criticism of behavior is sound criticism – no qualification is required. But the same does not seem true of law. If the grounds of legal obligation are somewhat arbitrary, and legal obligations are not automatically justifiable, then we cannot assume that the criticisms they warrant are valid, save in legal terms. If moral judgments of conduct are defensible, then a judgment based on moral considerations to the effect that one has acted wrongly is unqualifiedly true. But if legal criticisms of conduct can be justified by arbitrary standards, then we cannot infer that those judgments show that one has acted wrongly. To take morality seriously, we must suppose that immoral behavior is unqualifiedly wrong or bad. To take law seriously – to recognize that it establishes requirements and prohibitions on behavior – is not to suppose that unlawful behavior is wrong or bad, except in the eyes of the law.

If law is morally fallible, and moral judgments are capable of being sound, then we cannot regard morality and law as coordinate systems evaluating conduct. Legal criticisms must be taken with a grain of salt: it remains to be seen whether, in any particular context, the violation of law is in any respect a fault that is subject to sound criticism. That might be true in some cases, when law merits respect, but not in other cases, when law merits no respect at all.

The inner morality of law

Natural lawyers are sometimes said to believe that law is inherently good, right, and just. I do not know of any legal theorist who can fairly be understood to have believed this, and we have seen that Aquinas rejected the idea. Alternatively, natural lawyers have been said to claim that there are "necessary connections" between law and morality. This is a much broader doctrine. Some necessary connections between law and morality would not insure that law satisfies the moral standards by which it may properly be judged. But, if there were such connections, they might explain why law employs a vocabulary like that of morality. It might also explain what differentiates law from other social institutions with similar internal structures. We shall consider claims of this type now.

The American jurist Lon Fuller (1902–78) sketched one argument connecting law and morals, based on the purposive character of law.[29] Whatever else law may involve, it is used to regulate behavior. We do not have a system of law unless we have some norms that are supposed to be followed by those who are capable of following them. Moreover, law-making seeks to regulate behavior on a large scale. This requires general rules, not *ad hoc* legal decisions that are unpredictable. The rules must not be changed too frequently and must be interpreted by officials as they are reasonably understood by the people to whom they apply, or else they cannot be expected to provide regular guidance. They must be prospective, not retroactive, since no one can change behavior in the past. They must not entail inconsistent demands or require conduct beyond the powers of those they govern. Unless conditions like these are satisfied, law is incapable of achieving its essential function, that of providing general guidance for behavior which can actually be used by people to regulate their own conduct. If this is not accomplished, Fuller claims, we have something less than law.

That is what Fuller calls "the inner morality of law." The enterprise of regulating behavior by law generates principles that must be satisfied by those who govern, or else they fail to achieve that general purpose. These principles amount to an "internal" morality because they are implicit in the concept or nature of law. It is a "morality" because it provides standards for evaluating official conduct.

The inner morality of law requires that law be followable. This suggests another reason for considering its norms a "morality." It is generally considered unjust to penalize a person for failing to follow a law it is impossible to follow. Fairness requires that a person have fair warning – the opportunity to know what is expected of her and to decide what to do in light of that knowledge. Fuller can be understood to suggest, therefore, that certain principles of justice are implicit in the concept of law. This explains why law is not an "amoral datum" but an achievement always worthy of respect, however deficient it may be in other ways. If the inner morality of law is respected, certain forms of injustice will be avoided. Fuller thus suggests that law's inner morality accounts for an obligation of fidelity to law.

Fuller's theory can be seen as having three parts. One is the claim that certain principles are implicit in the concept of law. A second is that these principles constitute a morality. A third is that we lack law to the extent that these principles are violated (for that is clearly a matter of degree).

Fuller presents his view as a modern species of natural law, one that is exclusively "procedural" and not "substantive." He agrees that law is morally fallible. He holds, however, that law is followable. To the extent it is not followable, it does not count as law.

That claim seems false. Retroactive laws which provide criminal sanctions for conduct performed prior to their enactment may be unjust, but they seem no less laws for that. In a similar way, laws imposing "strict liability" make one subject to legal action for effects of one's conduct that one could not predict, and laws imposing "vicarious liability" make one subject to legal action for someone else's conduct not entirely under one's control. These may be objectionable, but they are no less laws for that.

One does not succeed in making law simply by providing guidelines for behavior – not even if he succeeds in channeling behavior as he desires. Something is not a law in isolation, but can be identified as law because of its place within a system of law. Unless the rules of a system were generally followed, we would not consider it a functioning legal system. And if they must be generally followed, they must be generally followable. But we cannot infer from this that each and every law within a system is followable. It seems a piece of arbitrary verbal legislation not to count unfollowable rules as law when they are normally counted as law. Fuller's third claim fails.

Fuller suggests another way of understanding his third claim. This is that a system which includes unfollowable rules lacks some of the quality of "legality." It is unclear what this should be taken to mean. If it simply means that the system is worse – less just – than it would be if all its rules were followable, then it amounts to a moral criticism of that body of law. But Fuller gives us no reason to suppose that the unjust body of rules is, for that reason, less a matter of *law*.

Fuller might reason as follows. If the rules of a system were unfollowable to a significant degree, it could not succeed in regulating behavior; and in that case, we would not *have* a body of law. From this he might infer that, to the degree that a system incorporates rules that are unfollowable, that system possesses less of the character of law. But that reasoning would be invalid. A man without hair is bald. It does not follow that a man who loses one hair is partly bald.

In any case, Fuller's second claim seems more relevant to our concerns. He regards the principles implicit in the law as a morality. But it is doubtful that the principles one can extract from the idea of law, as Fuller does, are moral standards in a relevant sense. To see this, we must go back another step and consider Fuller's first claim, that the purposive character of law generates principles that regulate the creation and administration of the law.

If one wishes to regulate behavior directly by means of general rules, then one must conform to principles like those Fuller describes. These are principles of social engineering. The idea that such principles are implicit in forms of human activity is not implausible. The same may be true, for example, of electrical engineering. But the same may also be true of warfare, professional assassination, slave-holding, and systematic genocide.

There may be a point in calling the principles that regulate such forms of human activity "moralities," but the term is misleading. For those principles would have no regular relations to fairness, justice, or other moral standards. They concern *effectiveness*, and we would not express them in moral terms. We have no reason to regard an assassin as violating moral principles because he is inept and unable to accomplish his murderous missions. Similarly, Fuller gives us no reason to believe that those who fail to make rules followable act unjustly.

If we think there is a connection between what Fuller calls

"the inner morality of law" and those moral standards by which the law may properly be judged, that is because we assume that unfollowable legal rules will be enforced. When a ruler acts unjustly because his rules are unfollowable, the injustice goes beyond this and includes his penalizing those who fail to follow the unfollowable rules. But this is *not* the defect in governance that Fuller identifies. Nor does he suggest how the *injustice* of enforcing unfollowable rules can be inferred from the concept of law. The defect in governance discussed by Fuller amounts to defeating one's presumed purposes. That may sometimes be regrettable, but it is not itself a matter of injustice. Fuller has failed to find any necessary connections between morality and law.

Though Fuller's argument seems to fail, we cannot conclude that his strategy is unsound. Other attempts have been made to find connections between the concept of law and moral standards. The most promising attempt is made, surprisingly, by Hart. Despite his suggestion that "there is no necessary connection between law and morals or law as it is and ought to be,"[30] he develops a theory of justice that is similar in one respect to Fuller's theory of law's inner morality. Hart claims to find a principle of justice implicit in the concept of law. Hart's theory is especially important because it provides a theoretical account of one of the most widely accepted ideas about the relations between law and morals.

The standard of strict adherence

Hart follows the venerable tradition of regarding justice as a matter of "treating like cases alike."[31] But this requires interpretation. There are innumerable ways in which cases may be classified as alike or different, since any arbitrary set of cases share some properties and fail to share others. Hart says, therefore, that the bare precept, "Treat like cases alike," must be supplemented by criteria determining when cases are alike or different.

We can go further. It also makes a difference how we treat the cases that fall into the classes we establish; for example, whether we reward good samaritans and punish rapists, or the contrary. A conception of justice requires not only a way of classifying cases but also guidelines for their respective treatment.

Ideas about justice vary, so different people have different ideas about what similarities and differences among cases are morally relevant and how various cases should be treated. If there are sound principles of justice, then not anything goes. Some ways of classifying cases and dealing with them are just and others are unjust.

Hart discusses two general contexts in which questions of justice arise. We judge the justice of laws, and we judge the justice of their application. This corresponds to the familiar distinction between "substantive" and "procedural" justice. Here we are chiefly concerned with the "procedural" aspect of Hart's theory of justice: the part that concerns justice in the application of the law to particular cases, or justice in the administration of the law.

In discussing the justice of laws, Hart rejects the implausible idea that justice amounts to conformity to law. We can intelligibly judge laws to be unjust and, Hart suggests, we sometimes do so soundly. If so, one who wishes to evaluate the law from the standpoint of justice must appeal to standards that law does not automatically respect. Hart assumes quite plausibly that these standards must be independent of the law. We may judge a law unjust because it discriminates between persons in a morally unacceptable way, as when blacks are treated with less respect than whites.

Hart believes, however, that this does not hold for justice in the application of the law to particular cases. Then *the law* provides the proper basis for deciding which cases are to be treated alike, which are to be treated differently, and how they are to be treated. This is Hart's conception of procedural justice: it requires strict adherence to the law (so far as that is possible).

Hart's theory of procedural justice has two parts. One is the standard of strict adherence to the law. This idea is pervasive within legal theory and merits discussion in its own right. The other part of Hart's position is that this principle of justice can be extracted from the concept of law. Because this amounts to the assertion of a "necessary connection" between law and a moral principle, it may be classified as a form of "natural law." In any case, many legal theorists seem to agree with Hart that such a principle follows from the concept of law, or at least from an application of the idea of treating like cases alike to the context of procedural justice. This aspect of Hart's theory merits careful scrutiny. It also helps explain how Hart, among others, understands the principle of justice in the administration of the law.

The standard of strict adherence implies that if an official fails to act within the law because he fails to deal with cases in the way the law prescribes, he acts unjustly. This must be qualified. As Hart and others recognize, justice concerns not only the administration of the law but also the laws themselves. The principles that may be used to judge laws may be relevant to official conduct in the following way. If a law is just, that presumably implies a strong moral reason to respect it. If a law is unjust, that presumably implies a strong moral reason not to respect it. If a law is sufficiently unjust, deviation from it may be justified – it may even be required – from a moral point of view. But the standard of strict adherence requires obedience to law, at least on the part of officials who are charged with applying it. This is compatible with the idea that morality might permit or even require deviation from the law, because the standard of strict adherence need not be considered "absolute." It can be overridden. In calling the standard of strict adherence a principle of justice, however, one implies that deviations from the law must be justified, and can be justified only in exceptional circumstances, by powerful moral considerations. Furthermore, if the standard makes any difference to the evaluation of official conduct, it must be capable of overriding conflicting moral considerations. If it has any moral teeth, it must imply that justice, overall, at least sometimes requires official adherence to the law even when the law is unjust or otherwise morally deficient.

The general idea of procedural justice and Hart's interpretation of it draw upon the important observation that injustice can be done not only by following the law but also by applying it unfairly. Consider a law that requires blacks to use separate public facilities. Because the facilities for blacks are inferior to those provided for whites, and in any case such segregation expresses official acceptance of the idea that blacks are inferior to whites, the law is unjust. Suppose that a black person is convicted under this law because he used a washroom reserved for whites. Since the law discriminates against blacks, this application amounts to an injustice. It is possible, however, for the injustice to be compounded by the way in which the law is applied to the particular case. The convicted black may be treated with unusual severity. He then suffers extra penalties and accordingly has two grounds for complaint: one for the injustice of being penalized under a discriminatory rule, the other for the injustice of being singled out on morally unacceptable grounds for special bad treatment.

Examples like these support the idea that injustice can be done not only by the laws themselves but also by the way they are applied. According to Hart's theory of procedural justice, they involve a conflict of moral principles. If the unjust law is enforced, an injustice is done. But, according to the standard of strict adherence, if the law is *not* enforced, an injustice is done. In such cases, officials are seen as faced with moral dilemmas. However one decides, an injustice will be done. It is possible that a judge or other official can be justified (from a moral, not a legal, point of view) in failing to follow the law. On Hart's view, that would presumably be the case if the injustice done in following the law would be worse than the injustice done in departing from it.

I shall argue that the standard of strict adherence is mistaken. I shall go on to suggest why something like it may be true in some cases, though not in all. But first I must explain why the standard of strict adherence is so strict.

Standard of SA
strict

Hart and others who embrace the standard apparently believe that the principle applies universally. I do not mean that they regard it as "absolute," as always taking precedence over other moral considerations. As we have seen, if they take into account the injustice of the law, they can allow that this principle may sometimes be broken, so as to avoid a worse injustice that would be done by following the law. But they believe that *a* principle of justice is violated whenever officials fail to follow the law that they are charged with administering. No other conditions are laid down for the application of this principle.

This goes considerably beyond the idea that justice in the application of the law is somewhat independent of justice in the laws themselves. From examples like the segregation case, we can see that injustice is done not only by following the law but also by applying it unfairly. That does not mean, however, that every deviation from the law by an official who is charged with administering it is an injustice, the breach of a sound moral principle, though Hart and others imply this. Let us now see how this comes about.

Hart supports the standard of strict adherence by suggesting that "to apply a law justly to different cases is simply to take seriously the assertion that what is to be applied in different cases is the same general rule, without prejudice, interest, or caprice."[32] He says furthermore, "So there is, in the very notion of law consisting of general rules, something which prevents us from treating it as if morally it is utterly neutral, without any necessary contact with moral principles."[33]

We might reconstruct Hart's undeveloped argument in the following way. Any system of law includes, of necessity, general rules. One cannot apply a general rule without deciding cases according to the criteria it lays down. In doing so, one treats a particular case which falls under the rule like other cases under the rule and unlike cases that do not fall under the rule; that is, one treats like cases alike according to the ways that are required by law. But justice consists in treating like cases alike. So in applying the law one is doing the sort of thing that justice requires. Thus, the very concept of law implies a principle of justice in the application of the law to particular cases. This principle is the standard of strict adherence to the law.

This argument is unsound. We began with the recognition that treating like cases alike needs interpretation, and that, if there are sound principles of justice, not anything goes. Not every way of dealing with cases in a uniform or regular manner is a way that is required, or even permitted, by justice. What Hart seems to show is that following the law amounts to a way of treating cases in a regular or uniform manner. But he does not show that treating cases in the way prescribed by the law is treating them in a way that is required, or even allowed, by a principle of justice, including a principle of procedural justice. Treating cases in a regular or uniform manner may be a necessary condition of justice, but it is not a sufficient condition. So from the fact that following the law involves treating cases in a regular or uniform manner we cannot infer that *any* sort of justice is thereby done.

This means that Hart's natural law argument fails. He has given us no good argument for the conclusion that "the very notion of law" has some "necessary contact with moral principles." Moreover, there is reason to believe that any such argument would fail. This is because the standard of strict adherence is not a sound principle of justice.

I do not mean that there are never any strong moral reasons for officials to follow the law. There may be good and sufficient reasons in many situations. But the standard of strict adherence oversimplifies the complex moral situation sometimes facing public officials.

Let us look more closely at the moral predicament of an official who is charged with administering an unjust law. In what we may regard as the normal case, someone who becomes an official is understood to assume a public trust. Though he may not believe that the law is morally impeccable, he has undertaken to apply the law as he finds it. He acquires an obligation of fidelity to the law, which he owes to the other members of the community who have placed this trust in him. When he is called on to enforce an unjust law, this obligation conflicts with an independent obligation to do justice, which implies that he should not allow himself to be an instrument of injustice. He faces a moral dilemma, a conflict of obligations.

So far, my description of the situation is parallel to that given by those who embrace the standard of strict adherence. But we part company now. I shall argue that the obligation of fidelity to law does not necessarily cover the case at hand.

In the first place, we cannot assume that a particular official has any moral obligation of fidelity to law. It depends, for example, on whether he has freely undertaken to administer the law. If an official has been coerced into serving by an oppressive regime that wishes to exploit his respected name, he has probably made no morally binding promise to be faithful to the law, even if he was forced to give his word. So from the fact that someone occupies a public office we cannot infer that he is morally bound to be faithful to the law. If so, an official charged with enforcing an unjust law may not be in a moral dilemma. He may run a personal risk if he wishes to subvert the unjust law, but his deviation from the law would not automatically violate a moral principle, no less a principle of justice.

There is another reason why an official's presumed obligation of fidelity to law may not apply to a case before him. The scope of such an obligation is not determined just by the law but also by moral considerations that are independent of the law. Consider parallel cases. A member of a social club may be under an obligation to participate in the group's chosen activities, as decided by majority vote; for this may be mutually understood within the group. But the obligation does not include a majority's decision to engage in a gang rape. A volunteer soldier may be under an obligation to obey his officers' commands, but this does not cover orders to murder acknowledged civilians. In such cases, it is not that the assumed obligation is overridden, but rather that it cannot be understood to extend so far – to require cooperation in deliberate, grossly immoral acts. So, even if an official has a general obligation of fidelity to law, we can assume it has moral bounds. If the law he is called on to enforce is sufficiently immoral, there may be no moral argument for his adherence to it – not even if he has sincerely undertaken to apply the law as he finds it. A misguided or naive official under the Third Reich, who initially believes that the law he shall be called on to administer will not be outrageously immoral, may find that it requires him to verify the eligibility of persons for extermination in the gas chambers because they are Jews. He may in good conscience have undertaken to apply the law as he finds it, but I see no reason to suppose that his resulting obligation of fidelity to law extends this far. Such an obligation has moral limits.

Let us apply this to the standard of strict adherence. We have found reason to question Hart's derivation of that principle from the concept of law. Now we have reason to doubt the principle itself. The principle asserts that any failure by an official to follow the law amounts to an injustice. The injustice might be justified by the need to prevent a worse injustice, but infidelity to law always violates an important principle. But – apart from Hart's invalid argument – why should we suppose that to be true? We might use the following test: if an injustice is supposed to be done, we should look for the victim of it. If no one suffers an injustice, then the claim that an injustice is done loses credence.

Suppose an official is charged with administering a segregation law. He realizes that by violating the rules of evidence he can avoid the legally prescribed application of the law. Suppose he does so. The standard of strict adherence implies that he acts unjustly. But let us try our test: to whom does he do an injustice? We cannot assume that he does an injustice to the person he fails to convict. (That might be plausible if the defendant wished to be convicted because, say, he wished to make a political point or to initiate a constitutional test of the law. But this will not always be true.) We cannot assume that he does an injustice to those who support the segregation law – those who wish to have blacks treated as inferior to whites. Frustrating their immoral purposes is no automatic injustice.

(We might be tempted to suppose that fairness requires us to defer to the law that they support, on the assumption that it resulted from a fair law-making process. But we cannot generally assume that legislative procedures have been fair. Some might believe this is true of our system. But we are not considering just our own system.) Perhaps it will be suggested that those who have in the past been convicted for violating the segregation law are done a further injustice now. For they have been treated differently from the way the defendant is being treated, although he did exactly what they did. This reasoning takes us to the heart of the claim that the standard of strict adherence is a principle of justice. It assumes that one principle of justice requires that cases be treated in a uniform or regular manner, even if the pattern already established is itself outrageously unjust or otherwise unconscionable.

To test such a claim, we must consider its implications in other cases, where our judgments may not be subtly influenced by assumptions about the moral character of the system as a whole. To argue in the way suggested is to imply that a German official who managed under the Nazi regime to save one Jew from the extermination camps by failing to follow the law he was charged with administering thereby did an injustice to those whom others had already sent to their deaths. I do not find that judgment at all plausible.

This argument is not meant to show that officials should always violate the law whenever it is not morally impeccable. Its point is that justice in the administration of the law is a much more complex matter than the standard of strict adherence allows. There are moral limits to the obligation of fidelity to law, just as there are to other obligations – limits which depend on the moral quality of the law, its social history, current circumstances, and the consequences of applying it.

Our discussion has neglected an important aspect of Hart's theory of justice in the application of the law to particular cases. We have taken for granted that the law to be applied is unproblematic – that it provides clear guidance for official decisions. So far as that is true, Hart's theory has the implications we have considered. But it is not always true. When the law is unclear, Hart's theory has quite different implications.

Let us look once more at what Hart says: "to apply a law justly to different cases is simply to take seriously the assertion that what is to be applied in different cases is the same general rule, without prejudice, interest, or caprice." In this and other ways Hart suggests that justice requires not merely following the law, but something more – applying it impartially.

If the meaning of the law is clear, determinate, and uncontroversial, so that it offers sufficient guidance for official decision, then there is only one way to act within the law, which is by following the law's directions. If all the law applicable to a case tells a judge that he must find for A rather than B, then the only way he can be faithful to the law is by rendering a decision that is favorable to A. In such a case, the requirement of impartiality is relevant *only* because a judge's lack of impartiality might prevent him from following the law. The requirement gives no guidance for decisions beyond what the law itself provides. When the law is clear, it must be followed. Anything that might deflect a judge from following the law is condemned on the same ground as bias or prejudice. This is reflected in Hart's formulation of the point.

Hart suggests, however, that in other cases impartiality has a larger role to play. When the law is unclear, judges cannot simply follow the law, but must go beyond it. Then the requirement of impartiality serves not merely as a negative constraint but as a more substantial guide to responsible judicial decision.

The area of "judicial discretion" constitutes a "window" through which moral standards might help determine what the law requires and allows. That is the topic to which we now turn.

The moral resolution of hard cases

Officials frequently seem faced with choices that leave room for discretion. Enforcement agencies must judge how best to use their limited resources. Prosecutors must decide which cases to pursue and which to bring to trial. Judges must set penalties under criminal statutes that establish maximum punishments but no minimum. Courts must determine how to apply unclear aspects of the law – which is especially important because it seems to reflect on the law itself.

If courts render authoritative interpretations of the law, but they have discretion to decide its meaning when it is unclear, then they do not simply apply the law. They also help to make it. They do not simply adjudicate: they also "legislate."

The language of ordinary legislation is understood by courts to fix the law, so far as it succeeds. But statutory language can be vague or ambiguous, and rules generated by legislation can appear to conflict or to leave legal questions unanswered. Then courts seem faced with the task of helping to shape the law.

In common law systems, where some law can be traced back not to legislation but only to judicial precedents, uncertainties about the law are multiplied. A judicial decision on a point of law is often framed to deal with a specific set of facts – to provide no more guidance than is required to settle the immediate issue. When other courts are guided by such decisions, they often must repeat the process; they must interpret the guidance offered by judicial precedents in order to decide cases that are somewhat different. Judicial decisions on points of law can thus be understood to work in two ways. They generate relatively narrow rules for cases that are just like those being decided. But they are also understood to have wider implications, covering cases that do not neatly fall under those narrow rules. These wider implications are often somewhat uncertain. The use of precedents reflects such uncertainty; different judges understand the wider implications of past cases differently. The same sort of uncertainty affects judicial interpretation of constitutional provisions and statutory enactments. Interpretive decisions are usually framed to deal with the narrowest legal issue that arises in a case. Their implications for further novel cases are then uncertain and often controversial.

I have described these circumstances in cautious terms, neither assuming nor denying that the law in problematic cases is not only unclear but also indeterminate, so that no particular decision is required by law.

In this section and the next, we shall consider two general approaches to problematic or "hard" cases. The first and more widely accepted view is defended most fully by Hart,[34] who emphasizes the limits of the law. The second and more recently developed view was presented initially by Ronald Dworkin. Our discussion will take up two questions. First, how should courts decide hard cases? Second, when courts decide hard cases in the way they generally ought to be decided, can they be understood to decide them *according to law*? These two questions are closely connected, but their connections will not emerge clearly until the next section.

Hart holds that a body of law amounts to a collection of rules, most of which (save for the most fundamental rules) are part of the system because they are "valid" according to the system's rules of recognition. Rules are general, in that they concern classes of acts that may be performed by individuals who belong to specified classes of persons. They have this general character because they are formulated in general terms, which apply to a wide range of situations that may differ in various ways. The meaning of a rule is determined by the terms used in legislation or in its standard formulation by the courts. General terms have a "core" of determinate meaning; that is, standard usage applies a given term uncontroversially to some cases and refrains from applying it to others. This gives rules their central core of meaning. But general terms are always somewhat vague, or "open textured"; that is, there are some actual or possible cases to which a term is neither standardly applied nor not applied. Hart calls this their "penumbra" of uncertain meaning, which affects the meaning of rules. So rules, like terms, are "open textured" too. Some cases can be decided by applying them, but other cases cannot be so decided.

Take for example an ordinance that prohibits vehicles from

public parks. It clearly excludes automobiles, trucks, and motorcycles (though exceptions may be made for emergency and service vehicles), but it does not clearly prohibit bicycles, skateboards, and other things that might or might not be thought of as "vehicles." If a case arises concerning the use within a public park of one of these problematic "vehicles," it cannot be decided by reference to the plain meaning of the ordinance. If a court is nevertheless required to decide the case (as often happens), it can do so only by going beyond the clear meaning of the ordinance and therefore only by appeal to considerations which are not given in the law.

The purpose of a rule may help decide a case.[35] If peace and safety in public parks are known to be objectives of the ordinance, then the ordinance cannot soundly be interpreted as excluding problematic "vehicles" that pose no threat to peace or safety in the parks. But purposes can be unclear, and they can conflict. So an appeal to the purposes of rules will not help decide all hard cases that might arise under them.

On this view, then, law has "gaps." Many cases can be decided by existing law, but some are undecidable at any given time. As problematic cases are decided by the courts, the doctrine of judicial precedent requires other courts in the same jurisdiction to decide similar cases in the same way. Then judicial decisions on hard cases make existing rules more determinate (in some cases they generate new rules, where none existed before) by a process that can be called "judicial legislation." But this process can never eliminate all gaps within the law, for it makes use of general terms, and the rules it generates will themselves be open textured too. Thus, a certain amount of "judicial discretion" is inevitable in a system of law; that is, cases can arise which cannot be decided by reference to existing law.

But courts are often called upon to decide hard cases. How should they proceed? Hart suggests one possible answer when he says that laws should be applied "without prejudice, interest, or caprice," which we have understood as a requirement of impartiality. As we have seen, Hart introduces this idea in connection with the application of rules, where their implications are assumed to be determinate. In such cases, the call for impartiality amounts to the requirement that judges not be deflected from following the law. When the law is unclear and (on Hart's view) indeterminate, the proper judicial role is more complex.

In discussing hard cases, Hart says that judges often "display characteristic judicial virtues ... impartiality and neutrality in surveying the alternatives; consideration for the interest of all who will be affected; and a concern to deploy some acceptable general principle as a reasoned basis for decision."[36] How should this be understood?

Against the background of Hart's theory of "judicial discretion," the question is how courts should decide cases that cannot be decided by existing law. What Hart seems to suggest is that courts should decide such cases in a morally responsible manner. Such a decision should be "principled." A court should base its decision on repeatable features of the case to be decided, for this enables the court to decide by appealing to general principles. But any case has innumerable features, only some of which can be used as the basis for decision. Which features should be taken as relevant depends on the general principles that should be used in deciding it.

The question before a court is how a hard case *should* be decided. A court can decide a case responsibly only by appealing to standards that are *capable* of determining what should be done. If the guidance of the law has been exhausted, this would seem to imply that courts should decide such cases by appealing to moral principles.

If this is assumed, then we can say that judges are duty-bound to decide hard cases by applying moral principles, because this is the only responsible way to proceed. Any failure to decide a hard case in that manner would be breach of judicial duty, a matter of judicial error.

This suggests another possible "necessary connection" between law and morality; that is, between law and those moral principles that judicial duty requires be used in deciding hard cases. How could this be defended? We must suppose that the judicial duty to decide hard cases in a morally responsible manner is somehow given by the very concept of law, or perhaps by the specific concept of the judicial role. The latter is a plausible suggestion. For it seems difficult to deny that courts are expected to decide cases in a morally responsible manner, or that this is an element of the judicial role. When the law is determinate, the division of legal labor that distinguishes adjudication from, say, legislation and enforcement seems to imply that courts should apply the law as they find it. In such cases, judges are not free to appeal directly to moral principles. But courts may be called upon to decide cases when there is not enough law to require a decision one way rather than another. If adjudication is still expected by its very nature to decide cases in a morally responsible manner, then it can do so only by applying moral principles. It must be admitted, however, that our concept of the proper judicial role is unclear in precisely those cases.

We shall not pursue this approach to hard cases further. That is because we must question the assumption that hard cases cannot be decided on the basis of existing law. The approach we have been considering may rest on false assumptions – about the logic of judicial reasoning and the limits of law.

The justification of judicial decisions

The approach to hard cases that we have just considered fits most naturally with a conception of law as a limited set of rules. This view of law reflects the fact that, in the societies with which we are most familiar, law is tied to complex institutions in which officials, such as legislators and judges, are authorized to make decisions which determine the law. Legislation is thought of as generating clear, specific rules – at least when it is properly done. Judicial precedents are understood to generate rules to deal with cases like those that are decided. Rules so generated are understood to serve as the basis for decisions grounded on existing law.

To complete the picture, we must add a model of judicial reasoning: the idea that a decision can be based on existing law when, but only when, a legal judgment can be established as the conclusion of a legal syllogism, which applies a clear, specific rule to a case in light of factual premises about it. On this view, law is applied just when judicial argument is strictly deductive, logically watertight. When cases cannot be so decided, adjudication goes beyond the limits of the law because it must go beyond the limits of clear, specific rules.

There are two problems with this picture. First, it does not seem to describe legal practice. Second, it seems to assume too restricted a model of reasoning that is capable of discovering facts.

When lawyers argue cases and courts decide them, their reasoning is not limited to the syllogistic application of clear, specific rules. They look behind the rules for purposes and "underlying principles." They consider policies that may be reflected in past decisions. If rules are unavailable, they look for guidance in decisions that deal with somewhat similar cases. In so reasoning, they do not act as if law was being created, by a process like legislation, transported to the courtroom. They speak and write as if they were discovering what the law requires and allows, even in hard cases.

Are these practices misleading? Or is it possible that law can be discovered even when it cannot be found in clear, specific rules which can be applied syllogistically? We are not entitled to ignore the facts of legal practice. These must be taken at face value until they are shown to be illusory.

We might think they are illusory if we take for granted the syllogistic model of judicial reasoning. But we cannot assume this model without special justification. In our everyday reasoning, as well as in our most rigorous scientific practice, we reach conclusions about matters of fact that are not entailed by the evidence. The evidence may point in different directions, so that our reasoning must take into account conflicting considerations. This reasoning is not syllogistic, deductive, logically watertight. But this does not mean, nor do we usually take it to mean, that our conclusions are groundless or that there is no matter of fact to be discovered. The idea, that there is no matter of fact unless it can be proved by watertight reasoning from certain premises, seems indefensible outside the law, and it is unclear why we should impose such a model on the law. What law requires and allows may be determined not simply by the mechanical application of clear, specific rules, but also by the weight of legal argument favoring one side rather than another.

The problem in hard cases is not usually a dearth of law but an excess of guidance from past decisions. It is not that law has been exhausted, but that clear, specific rules appear incapable of determining sound decisions, either because such rules do not cover the case at hand or else because there are significant objections, grounded in law, to so interpreting the law. We must therefore entertain the possibility that there is more content to law than what can be deduced from clear, specific rules.

Consider the case of *Riggs* v. *Palmer*.[37] Elmer Palmer murdered his grandfather in order to inherit his property. Although convicted of the crime, Palmer still seemed eligible to inherit under his grandfather's will, because the statute governing wills made no exception for such a case. Other relatives challenged this interpretation of the law, and the courts agreed with their contention.

If the relevant law consisted solely of the rules that could be inferred from the language of the statute, then there would be no room for further legal argument. But the court did not assume this. It considered the purpose of the statute, the relevance of a number of other cases, and the judicial practice of "equitable construction," especially in light of the common law maxim that no one shall be permitted to profit from his own wrong. The dissenting member of the court did not object to this general approach. He argued that the statute must be read more strictly because it was worded in a way that seemed to prohibit such an exception.

The *Riggs* opinions are not unusual. They imply that there is more to law than clear, specific rules which are strictly entailed by the wording of statutes and judicial precedents. They imply that statutes as well as past judicial decisions are subject to interpretation, and that there are no rigid boundaries to the arguments which might be marshaled on one side or another.

The question that we face is whether systematic sense can be made of such legal practice. We shall consider a theory that tries to accomplish this – to explain how decisions can be based on existing law even when they cannot be derived syllogistically from clear, specific rules. The theory we shall consider was first suggested by Ronald Dworkin and later by Neil MacCormick.[38] Although these writers disagree about the merits of legal positivism, their views about hard cases are somewhat similar. We shall ignore their differences (as well as many details of their developed theories) and shall sketch a theory of hard cases, based on their work, which emphasizes the role of moral principles in adjudication and suggests another "necessary connection" between morality and law.

If a theory of hard cases is to make sense of actual practice, it must explain how legal argument can go beyond the application of clear, specific rules and yet be grounded on established law. How might this work? Some possible answers are too vague. It is sometimes said, for example, that judges reason "by analogy" from past decisions. But this is unclear; it also suggests that courts can decide hard cases only by unsystematic extrapolations from existing law. Other possible answers will not serve our theoretical purposes. One might argue, for example, that law contains, besides clear, specific rules, some looser principles that are regularly referred to by the courts. This would account for the *Riggs* court's use of the common law maxim that no one shall be permitted to profit from his own wrong, for example, but it would suggest no special connection between morality and law, for it implies that such a principle has legal standing only by virtue of its past use by the courts.

The theory to be sketched offers a different kind of answer. It claims that various strategies of argument applied to hard cases can best be understood as regulated by the principle of fairness, that like cases be treated alike. This explanation is supposed to provide the best explanation of the best judicial practice. Since it is claimed to make good sense of actual practice, which implies that law is discovered, not made, in hard cases, the theory may be understood to show how a moral principle (fairness) helps generate decisions that can be justified by existing law. Let us now consider what the theory says about hard cases in two different contexts.

When hard cases arise under legislation, courts typically make reference to the "intentions" of the legislature. But this is misleading. Courts are not generally concerned with psychological facts about the members of the legislature, why individuals voted as they did, what they had in mind at the time, and the like. This is not just because the historical record is incomplete. It is chiefly because some historical facts about the legislature are irrelevant to a court's proper concerns when it interprets legislation.

Courts often take into account the actual history of legislation, which sometimes reveals clear reasons for specific enactments. Beyond that, however, they interpret legislation on the regulative principle that it should be construed, if at all possible, as a *reasonable* means to achieve some *reasonable* goals.

This can be understood in the following way. In a hard case, a court must seek a *justified* decision. But a satisfactory justification must develop within the constraints imposed by law – in this case, chiefly, by the legislative decision to enact a particular statute. The problem is how to interpret the legislative act so as to decide the case at hand. If a hard case can be decided on the *very same* grounds that could be used to *justify* the original legislation, then it can be decided on grounds that are *both* constrained by the legislative act *and* capable of justifying a decision. A court's reference to the "intentions" of the legislature can be understood as the search for principles and policies that justify the original legislation. So reasoning, a court can claim to decide the case on the best construction to be placed on that legislation. At the same time, it can claim to be respecting the principle that like cases be treated alike, for the hard case is decided on the same grounds that may be said to "underlie" the original legislation, where the "underlying" relation is not a mere matter of historical fact but a normative matter, involving justification.

Suppose, for example, that a legislature enacts a law prohibiting any reference to racial and sexual distinctions in agencies, and a court must decide whether this outlaws or permits "affirmative action" programs, which give preference in hiring to women and others, within groups that suffered systematic discrimination. In deciding such a case, a court must determine whether the statute should be understood as, say, prohibiting any reference to racial and sexual distinctions in hiring policies or, alternatively, as a means of rectifying past injustices, which might also require actively recruiting members of those groups which had been subject to discrimination. To some extent, this decision may be based on the actual history of the legislation, including arguments advanced for it. But the record may be unclear, and in any case the court must consider the best construction to be placed on the statute. Other things being equal, if one set of arguments for the statute is stronger than the other, that is the construction to prefer.

Interpretive arguments like these will be complex and controversial. They must take into account not only the justification that might be given the particular statute but also the proper interpretation to be placed on other aspects of the law, such as related statutes and constitutional provisions. But neither the complexity of the arguments nor the controversiality of the results shows that there is no best interpretation of such a law. On the theory we are now considering, to determine the best interpretation of the law *is* to discover what the law requires and allows. Legal arguments will always be available in support of alternative interpretations of the law, but this only shows that interpretive arguments cannot be deductively watertight. It does not show that there is no legal fact of the matter to be discovered.

   Past judicial decisions are also appealed to for guidance in deciding cases. As we have seen, hard cases arise because precedents can be understood to have wide as well as narrow implications. They generate clear, specific rules governing cases just like those already decided, but they are also relevent to a wider range of cases, which are somewhat like but also somewhat unlike the cases already decided. If past decisions represent more law than the narrow rules they clearly generate, appeal must go beyond those rules, to the considerations that provide the best justification for the judicial precedents.

   Suppose, for example, that a court must decide whether to hold Alice liable for doing an act of type X, and it appeals to a decision in which Claudia was held liable for doing an act of type Y. The court might use the previous decision for guidance in the new case if the previous decision represents the application of a *broader* principle, to the effect that one is liable for an act of type Z, where X and Y are species of the genus Z. This broader principle need not have been cited by the court that ruled in the previous case (though that would make the present court's justificatory argument easier). The broader principle must, however, provide the best justification for the previous decision.

   Actual decisions in hard cases are typically more complex than this schematic example might suggest. Not only are past decisions subject to alternative interpretations, based on alternative justifications that might be given for them, but often more than one judicial precedent seems relevant to a novel case. As a consequence, many arguments are available to counsel on either side. These arguments must be evaluated by the court. Alternative interpretations must be weighed, and the competing principles and policies that can be found to justify past decisions must be weighed against one another.

   This need not be thought of as an irrationally "intuitive" process. For various further considerations are available. Though a new case may resemble a previous case, some of the interests now at stake may be much slighter than those balanced in the previous case, so that its rationale should now be assigned less weight. Some principles or policies are more important in the system as a whole because they are required to justify vast areas of law that are taken as relatively settled and unproblematic. Thus, for various related reasons courts will tend to respect the explicit provisions of contracts and wills even when there are significant moral objections to doing so in the case to be decided.

This theory may now be summarized as follows. It claims, first, that legal reasoning, like reasoning outside the law, can be sound – can deal with legal matters of fact that are subject to discovery – even though it does not simply apply hard and fast rules. Sound legal arguments, like arguments outside the law, can take into account conflicting considerations and give them their due weight, in view of the specific facts and the relevant standards.

But what standards are relevant, beyond clear, specific rules? In easy cases, the application of rules is supposed to justify judicial decisions. If decisions can be justified in hard cases, that must be done differently. Judicial argument is supposed to apply the law – to carry it forward – not make it up as one goes along. This represents the idea of "justice according to law," which requires fairness in the sense of treating like cases alike – treating new cases on the same basis as past cases. How can one respect this principle and at the same time base one's decisions on decisions that have been made in the past? In hard cases, this cannot be done by reapplying hard and fast rules. But it *can* be done by reapplying considerations that "underlie" past decisions, in a sense that permits and, indeed, requires their continued application. If we understand the interpretation of legislation and judicial precedents, which involves the search for "underlying" principles and policies, as seeking to identify standards that provide the best justification for those decisions, then this approach to hard cases enables us to accomplish three things at once. It *provides a criterion* for identifying relevant standards beyond clearly established rules. The standards so identified must be *capable of justifying* decisions. They are the sort of standard that *serves the purpose of the fairness principle*, that is, the sort one would wish to carry forward in treating like cases alike. If alternative interpetations of past decisions are possible, and these correspond to different ways of deciding a current hard case, then presumably the *best* interpretation of a past decision – the one we would wish to use as the basis for deciding a current case, within the constraints of the fairness principle – is one in terms of the best justification of the past decision.

This sort of theory therefore suggests how law can be discovered in hard cases, and it makes that discovery depend on moral considerations – the fairness of treating like cases alike and the justification of judicial decisions. But these moral considerations likewise serve as constraints on legal discovery. Past legislative and judicial decisions can serve as bases for decisions in hard cases *only if and when* those past decisions *are* justifiable, and only within the limits of an argument from fairness.

If hard cases arise under segregation statutes, for example, and those statutes are unjustifiable, then those cases cannot be decided by reference to principles or policies that are capable of justifying the statutes. In that event, the theory of hard cases we have sketched provides no guidance for the courts. For the theory assumes that past legislative and judicial decisions are justifiable, and it interprets those decisions in terms of the standards that are capable of justifying them. Such cases may then be decided by the courts, but – according to the theory we are now considering – those decisions cannot be grounded on existing law. That is because those decisions cannot be justified in the way the theory requires.

This suggests a general problem for this sort of theory. If law is limited to decisions that can be justified, then this will affect our ideas about easy cases, that is, cases that are supposed to be decidable by the more or less mechanical application of rules. Consider the following sort of case. Suppose that a legal system enforces severely discriminatory laws against blacks. As a way of trying to insure the stability of the system, the law provides that a white may claim damages from any black who publicly challenges his racial superiority. Suppose that a case has arisen in which there is ample evidence, admissible in law, to support a particular white man's claim for damages against a particular black man under this law. The decision that would seem to be required by law would vindicate this white man's claim and require the black man to pay him compensation for the supposed injury. Let us assume, finally, that this law cannot be nullified on constitutional grounds.

I see no reason to suppose that any facts so far cited could justify such a decision. It may be argued, however, that the decision that seems required by law is justifiable precisely because it is required by law. This requires us to consider the notion of justification more closely.

The application of the law is not a purely intellectual exercise which results in merely labeling some behavior as "lawful" or "unlawful" or the like. Law's application affects substantial interests in important ways. In the name of the law, people are treated in ways that would not otherwise be considered justifiable. Punishments may be imposed. Enforceable orders may be issued, backed by the force of the state. Damages may be assessed. To justify a judicial decision, then, is typically to justify treating people in ways that require justification, such as depriving them of life, freedom, or valuable goods.

Sometimes specific decisions can be justified on their merits, as, say, fair settlements of disputes. But we cannot assume that this is always possible, as in the case we are now considering. In any event, judicial decisions are generally based on standards that are considered binding on the courts. The justification of a decision may then turn upon the justification of the standards that are applied. But, if law is morally fallible, then the standards that courts are called on to apply may themselves be unjustifiable. In that case, the justification of a decision depends on there being a justification for *following* a standard, such as a statute, which is *not itself* justifiable.

It is often claimed that judicial decisions can be justified when they are required by clear, specific rules that have been generated by past legislative or judicial decisions. If law is morally fallible, this assumes that the practice of following established rules is justifiable *even when* the rules themselves are not. But a justification of this practice presupposes further values that are supposedly served, and we cannot assume that those values are effectively served no matter how bad established rules may happen to be. If a system is sufficiently unjust, the practice of following its established rules may not be justifiable.

Here is where the principle of fairness may be assumed to do its work. We need not assume that fairness is the only value to be served. We need only assume that judicial respect for established rules is required by the principle of fairness, in the way that a single principle may require a certain course of action, even though other principles argue to the contrary. The argument from fairness suggests that, despite the moral deficiencies of past legislative and judicial decisions and the rules they have generated, there is always a good (though not, perhaps, a conclusive) reason for following them.

But I see no reason to suppose that fairness requires, or even allows, that established rules be followed, *regardless* of how bad they might be. Consider the case at hand. Let us suppose that the law which permits whites to claim damages from blacks who have publicly challenged their racial superiority has been applied to a number of cases in the past, and that judgments have always been handed down which scrupulously followed that law. If fairness were to make a difference in the way suggested, then it must make a difference here. We should be able to understand how an argument from fairness provides some justification for a decision against the black man, on the ground that it amounts to treating like cases alike. But I see no plausibility in that suggestion. The idea that we should continue to deal with cases as we have dealt with them in the past may make a difference in some cases, but it cannot be assumed to have unlimited application. Its plausibility varies inversely with the immorality of past decisions. If past decisions were sufficiently outrageous, then like cases *should not* be treated alike.

But the idea that decisions can be justified when they are required by established rules might still be salvaged. One might relax the notion of justification so that some kind of "justification" is *always* available for legislative and judicial decisions. This would make it possible to "justify" decisions in both hard and easy cases on the basis of established rules or whatever standards can be counted as "justifying" the decisions that generated them. A legislature might believe, for example, that segregation laws are necessary to prevent the "pollution" of one race by others, or that segregation is required to secure peace in the community. If arguments like these can count as "justifying" such legislation, *even when they are unsound*, then "justification" will be more generally available, though the notion of justification will then be interpreted in more or less arbitrary terms, based on, say, the values of those who wield power in the community.

If the argument from fairness is limited in the way suggested earlier, so that it does *not* require adherence to established rules *regardless* of their merits, then the idea that decisions based on established rules can always be justified, at least to some extent, requires such a weakened notion of "justification." If we relax the notion of justification in this way, then we can do the same with the principle of fairness. We can assume that "fairness" requires that like cases be treated alike, regardless of how they have been treated in the past. This would permit the theory of hard cases to guide decisions even when past legislative and judicial decisions could not be justified. For it assumes that they could be "justified" by some standards or other, and that "fairness" requires deciding novel cases by applying those underlying standards.

A theory of hard cases can therefore be interpreted and developed in different ways, depending on which notion of justification it uses. The first notion of justification that we used has moral significance, but the second does not. The first use assumes that the arguments available for particular decisions rest ultimately on standards by which law can properly be judged. But the second use of "justification" – the one it seems appropriate to place within quotation marks – permits "justification" to rest ultimately on unsound or arbitrary premises.

The alternatives reflect the fact that such a theory of hard cases is pulled in two directions. If we emphasize the need to justify decisions, then we shall find ourselves limited by the moral fallibility of law. If we emphasize the role of institutional decisions, regardless of their merit, then we shall find it difficult to justify decisions so grounded, except in an eviscerated sense of "justification."

The moral seems to be this. If hard cases can be decided by reference to existing law, then those decisions will by and large reflect the merits and demerits of that law. If so, then a theory of hard cases fails to reveal a significant connection between morality and law. Moral principles may help to shape the law, but they cannot be assumed to do so any more effectively than they do the rest of the law.

The moral neutrality of law

Our discussion of the relations between morality and law began with the idea that law is morally fallible – that law is subject to moral appraisal but does not automatically satisfy the standards by which it may properly be judged. Understood weakly enough, so that it simply acknowledges the possibility of bad and unjust law, this idea serves as a constraint on legal theory. It does not exclude the possibility that law has a moral dimension, but it does limit the ways in which morality may be thought to shape the law.

We have considered several arguments suggesting that law is shaped by moral conditions or has inherent moral content. We have considered the shared vocabulary of law and morals, the possibility that moral standards might be implicit in the idea of law, and the role of moral reasoning in deciding hard cases. Each suggestion seemed to fail.

We seem left with the following conclusion: the existence

and content of law is determined by facts that make law subject to moral appraisal but do not guarantee it any moral value. The connections between law and sound moral principles (if there are any) are not necessary but contingent. Law is, in this sense, morally neutral.

Many who think of themselves as legal positivists would agree that law is morally neutral. But it is unclear that positivists have done so consistently, or that this can serve as a basis for distinguishing legal positivism from natural law. Aquinas, for example, seems to agree that (human) law is morally neutral. He accordingly believes we have no automatic moral obligation to obey laws made by human beings. Legal obligations have no automatic moral force.

Legal positivists are unclear about this issue because they often suggest that law has automatic moral force. Kelsen, for example, appears to believe that no sense can be made of the notion that law is either just or unjust; for justice, he says, is an "irrational" ideal. This reflects his ethical nihilism. Despite this, however, he endorses a view like Hart's, that justice requires obedience to law.[39] Kelsen seems to believe that law (*un*like morality) merits our respect. Bentham, by contrast, is no ethical nihilist. He believes that law is morally fallible. He also believes that resistance to established government and its laws can sometimes be justified. But he holds that "under a government of laws" a "good citizen" will "obey punctually."[40] He assumes that there is normally good reason for fidelity to law. Hart seems to agree. Though he, along with Austin and others, regards law as morally fallible, he understands legal obligation so that it seems to merit as much respect as moral obligation.

Dworkin sometimes seems to regard law as morally neutral. In developing his theory of hard cases, he says, for example, "The constitution sets out a general political scheme that is sufficiently just to be taken as settled for reasons of fairness."[41] This implies that certain moral conditions must be satisfied for his theory to apply. If a system is "sufficiently just to be taken as settled for reasons of fairness," then we have a moral argument for carrying law forward – an argument that might justify the application of the law even when it is morally deficient. But not otherwise. Fairness does *not* require that we continue to treat cases as they have been treated before, if they have been treated in an outrageously unjust manner.

When a system is "sufficiently just," law serves as a set of moral constraints upon decision-making. It is not that each and every norm within the system can be justified on its merits, but rather that the system's practice of deciding cases by reference to established norms can itself be justified.

The general idea is not unfamiliar. In our private lives we accept the notion that we are bound by our own freely made decisions, even when they are not maximally enlightened, just, or wise but have unexpected, unfortunate consequences. We make promises, establish special relationships, accept jobs, and must decide what to do in the light of those commitments, which serve as constraints on how we may in good conscience proceed. In many situations our choices are also constrained by decisions that others have made, even after we have made our original commitments. This occurs in private clubs and other associations, in business firms and universities. The same applies to law.

This does not mean that law ever exhausts all moral considerations that may be relevant to a decision. Because law is morally fallible, there is always the possibility of a conflict between what the law requires in a case and what morality otherwise requires. When law has moral force, such a conflict generates a moral dilemma.

This can be understood as follows. Justifying a judicial decision is like establishing a distinct moral obligation. When the application of the law can be justified, the obligation so established is capable of conflicting with rights and duties that are independent of the law. A private citizen or an official might then be justified in departing from the law, but only when her legally based obligations are outweighed by other moral obligations.

However, Dworkin sometimes suggests a different view of

law. He explicitly considers law under regimes that one might think are *not* "sufficiently just to be taken as settled for reasons of fairness" – Nazi Germany and contemporary South Africa. He seems to say that law, even in such systems, generates "genuine" rights and obligations, which are capable of conflicting with rights and duties that are totally independent of the law.[42] This is puzzling.

One possible explanation of Dworkin's claim that law always generates genuine rights and duties is that he assumes justice and fairness are matters of degree. The more just a system, the stronger considerations of fairness argue for carrying law forward and respecting legal rights and duties. We can add that the injustice in a system is likely to be unevenly distributed. While some parts of a body of law may be outrageously unjust, other parts may be perfectly defensible.

Consider law in the United States prior to 1865, when the Thirteenth Amendment, which abolished chattel slavery, was added to the US Constitution. While it seems reasonable to hold that laws enforcing slavery could not be justified, it can be assumed that this aspect of the law did not render all the rest unjustifiable. Though laws enforcing slavery had effects throughout the law, they did not infect every corner. So, even if a system is not in all respects "sufficiently just to be taken as settled for reasons of fairness," some parts of it may be. Those parts of the law may be capable of generating "genuine" rights and obligations.

But reasoning like this will not show what Dworkin seems to imply – that all clearly established legal rights and duties are capable of conflicting with independent moral rights and duties. Laws enforcing slavery, for example, seem to generate rights and duties that are merely legal, devoid of moral force.

Dworkin suggests another reason for his view of legal rights and duties. Justification of the law or of decisions taken under it appeals to values that are accepted by those governed by the law.[43] This reflects a theory of justification, not a claim about any particular system. If people are committed to the values embodied in the system, the application of the law can then be justified, at least as a moral constraint on decisions.

Dworkin seems to assume that the basic principles and policies reflected in a legal system can be attributed to the community as a whole. Even if we make this assumption, however, and take for granted Dworkin's suggested theory of justification, we cannot infer that law has automatic moral force. For we cannot assume that the treatment of an individual that is prescribed by law accords with *her* own values. Communities are typically complex and heterogeneous. We cannot assume that the fundamental values reflected in a legal system are shared by all who are subject to its governance. In some circumstances, slaves might accept the basic values that justify the legal enforcement of slavery. But it is implausible to suppose that this must always be the case. If so, it may be impossible to justify the application of laws enforcing slavery against slaves.

But if decisions truly made in the name of the law cannot be justified, then the corresponding legal rights and duties have no moral force. There may be sound prudential reasons for complying with the law, but no trace of moral fault may lie with those who resist.

The rule of law seems to provide a possible framework for just social conditions – a *necessary* condition of justice in at least some social circumstances. Consider in this context the idea of treating like cases alike. If treating cases in a morally responsible manner means (among other things) dealing with them in a regular, uniform way, then the precept, "Treat like cases alike," can be understood to express a necessary condition of justice. If justice in a community means (among other things) settling conflicts and deciding issues in a regular, uniform manner, then, so far as the rule of law requires regular, uniform decisions, it can be understood to satisfy a necessary condition of justice. The rule of law takes us *part* way toward morality. This is not insignificant – but neither should it be exaggerated. A necessary condition of justice is one thing; justice is much more.

One reason we had for considering possible connections between law and morality was the inadequacy of existing social theories of law. This led us to wonder whether law might be distinguished from other institutions by reference to its moral dimension. It seems on reflection, however, that this is not very likely. For the clearest features of law, such as the complex internal structure explored by Hart, are by no means peculiar to law, while the features of law that seem the most plausible bases for its distinctness, such as its alleged "monopoly" on force, do not suggest properties of inherent moral value.

This last point suggests that moral problems will continue to be generated by the existence of human law. Law typically uses coercion and direct force to regulate behavior in a community. It orders people about, restricts their choices, deprives them of liberty and sometimes even of life. We must now consider how such practices might be justified.

4

Welfare, justice, and distribution

We now turn from the analysis of law to "normative" jurisprudence – from the nature of law to its evaluation. In this chapter we will examine some general normative theories. We shall begin with utilitarianism, which takes human welfare as its value, and then turn to a theory of justice that challenges utilitarianism.

Although our primary concern is the evaluation of law, these theories have wider implications. A broad perspective seems appropriate because the law provides wide possibilities of deliberate intervention in social arrangements. To the extent that the conditions under which we live are subject to moral appraisal and are susceptible to control by legal action, law is accountable for our fates. The law has indirect as well as direct impact on our lives. We are concerned here with general principles for appraising that impact.

This chapter will serve three purposes. It will explain some moral ideas that have practical and theoretical, contemporary and historical importance. By appraising these ideas, it will complement our discussion of moral judgments and their justification. It will also lay the groundwork for the chapters to follow. Utilitarianism, for example, is an important view about the legal use of coercion and legitimate limitations on personal freedom.

The plausibility of utilitarianism

Utilitarianism is a "normative" theory. In the context of moral philosophy, this does not mean that it claims to describe how decisions are "normally" made, but rather that it lays down a standard for appraising and guiding conduct. Utilitarianism takes many forms, but the central idea of its most common and traditional forms is that acts and institutions must be judged solely by their effects on human *welfare,* where the welfare of an individual is understood to be determined by facts about that individual's interests, wants, and needs. A person is assumed to be better off when her interests, wants, and needs are satisfied, and worse off when they are frustrated. Thus, utilitarianism may be understood as a theory which claims that decisions should promote the *good* of those who are affected by them, and which adds to this a conception of human good in terms of welfare.

In its traditional forms, utilitarianism judges institutions indirectly, since the direct subject of evaluation is human action or decision. As institutions are subject to control by human beings, especially in a legal context, they fall under the utilitarian principle because we can make decisions that affect the establishment, modification, or maintenance of institutions.

To understand utilitarianism better, it may be useful to contrast it with the principle of "prudence." Prudence evaluates actions or decisions in relation to the *agent's* own good or welfare. A person acts prudently when she serves her own best interests; she acts imprudently otherwise. Prudence may or may not require that one serve *others'* welfare; it requires that one do so only as a way of serving one's own welfare most effectively. For this reason, prudence is not usually regarded as a moral standard. Utilitarianism, by contrast, evaluates actions or decisions in relation to the *general* welfare. It requires us to take others' welfare into account and to serve welfare generally, to the maximum degree possible.

Just as a prudent person will often be unable to serve all of her interests, wants, and needs, but must sacrifice some that are less important in order to serve others that are more important, an individual who follows the dictates of utility will often be unable to serve everyone's welfare to the same degree. Just as prudence counsels an individual to serve her own best interests in the long run, utilitarianism requires that one act so as to promote welfare generally, to the maximum degree, in the long run. When the interests of a given individual conflict, prudence says that individual should serve her own greater aggregate interest. When the interests of different individuals conflict, utilitarianism says that we should serve the greater aggregate interest, taking into account all the benefits and burdens that might result from the decisions that are available to us.

This assumes that the relevant effects of acts on different individuals can be compared quantitatively. How this can be done, indeed whether it can be done at all, is theoretically controversial. Those who hold that "interpersonal comparisons of utility" are impossible, but who believe that something like utilitarianism is a sound normative theory, substitute some notion of "economic efficiency" (so called because of its role in economic theory) for the requirement that welfare be maximized. The resulting theories are similar to utilitarianism in many ways, and for our purposes the differences can be ignored.

Bentham believed that welfare can be measured by the intensity and duration of "pleasure" and "pain," which he took to be aspects of conscious experience when one's desires are realized and frustrated, respectively. Later theorists, seeking an uncontroversially public basis for utilitarian calculations, and worried about the "privacy" of pleasure and pain, developed the theory in terms of the satisfaction and frustration of preferences that people might exhibit in situations of choice.

Utilitarians usually assume that welfare is determined by the actual desires or preferences that people happen to have. But some believe that actual desires and preferences can be unreliable guides to welfare. It makes sense to suppose, for example, that satisfying some actual desires or preferences would make a person worse off than she might otherwise be, because specific desires and preferences can be based on mistaken beliefs about the consequences of action. This leads some utilitarians to rely on a more "objective" conception of human welfare, based on deeper or more permanent desires or preferences. Utilitarians have sometimes gone further and suggested that what is good or bad for the individual is not an ordinary fact about an individual but something that can only be discovered by value judgments about the good life. Such reasoning leads away from traditional utilitarianism, which holds that private and public decisions should be regulated by calculations based on ordinary, observable facts about people. Moral questions are understood by this theory to be objectively decidable, on the basis of ascertainable facts. Many find this feature of utilitarianism a clear mark in its favor.

Utilitarianism, as a moral theory, has often been associated with doctrines from which it should be distinguished, so that the merits and demerits of those doctrines will not be taken to reflect on utilitarianism. A few examples are worth mentioning here. Some utilitarians have assumed that people are naturally self-centered – a doctrine called "psychological egoism." But utilitarianism itself is a theory about how decisions *should* be made, not about how decisions are in fact made. Moreover, as utilitarianism requires that one take others' welfare into account, it may be incompatible with any psychological theory which implies that cannot generally be done. It is sometimes suggested that utilitarianism is committed to a free market system within a capitalistic economy. But this does not follow directly from utilitarianism, and might also be incompatible with it. A consistent utilitarian will advocate a particular economic or political system only if he believes it is likely to serve the general welfare most effectively, taking everyone's interests into account. Utilitarians have traditionally been concerned with institutional reform, on the plausible ground that the general welfare would be much better served by different arrangements. Utilitarianism is sometimes presented so that it seems to be concerned with the welfare of those within only one community (the community whose institutions it is currently evaluating). But this ignores the interests of those outside the community who may be affected by its decisions. A different understanding of utilitarianism seems more faithful to that tradition: it is concerned with the welfare of all people, regardless of political or other boundaries. Calculations based on narrow national interests are no more faithful to utilitarianism than are those based on purely selfish interest. (Since animals other than human beings have interests too, some utilitarians would also take their interests into account, but that is a complication we shall ignore.) This does not mean that all should be treated exactly alike, but rather that "everybody is to count for one, nobody for more than one."[44] Each person's welfare is to be included in our calculations; no one's may be discounted. Finally, utilitarianism should not be confused with any form of "cost-benefit analysis" which can be predicated on serving any arbitrary end whatsoever or which assumes that all interests are translatable into cash value. Utilitarian calculations are based on the service of human welfare: nothing more – but nothing less either.

It seems difficult to deny that human welfare is *relevant* to moral judgment. Some have thought this too obvious to require argument. But, even if welfare is *a* basic value, why should we suppose that it is *the single* fundamental value? We shall now consider some lines of reasoning that have been suggested for utilitarianism.

Some utilitarians believe that their theory expresses a commitment to benevolence in its most consistent and thoroughgoing form. One who lives by its dictates manifests a concern for all human beings. As benevolence is considered a moral virtue, this might be taken as an argument for utilitarianism. It does not tell us, however, why we should regard benevolence as the most basic moral attitude – more important than, say, a concern for justice – or why we should adopt any such attitude at all.

Problem

It often seems to be assumed that prudence is the only rational basis for decision. If that were the case, it would seem irrational to try to serve the general welfare when that conflicts with one's own best interests in the long run. To meet this challenge, utilitarians have sometimes suggested that, given the interdependence of human beings, conflicts of interest between persons are not fundamental and that our interests are best served all together. But this is difficult to defend. While conflicts of interest may often be exaggerated, they seem hard to deny.

Utilitarians have sometimes suggested another way of dealing with the plausibility of prudence. They have suggested that utilitarianism, rather than prudence, captures the underlying notion that makes prudence plausible. One such argument may be sketched as follows. Prudence says that, if an act would serve my welfare, then I have good reason to perform it, and if an act would undermine my welfare (or would serve it less than is otherwise possible), then I have good reason against performing it. But, if the fact that an act would serve my welfare gives me good reason to perform it, then so does the fact that an act would serve someone else's welfare. For (the argument claims) what underlies prudence is the connection between an action and *someone*'s welfare, not *my* welfare in particular. This can be inferred from the fact that I do not have good reason to serve just any arbitrary end whatsoever, but (according to prudence) only welfare. If prudence is a sound normative consideration, therefore, then so is the generalization of it – the principle that requires one to serve welfare in general.

It is unclear that this argument succeeds. Critics contend that prudence is a fundamental principle, one that does not rest on the idea that welfare should more generally be served. Prudence is a rational principle because the promotion and protection of one's own welfare is a criterion of rational behavior. At least when other interests are not at stake, one who neglects her own interests acts irrationally. If this is right, then the argument fails. That would not show, of course, that utilitarianism is mistaken or unfounded, for it might be justifiable on other grounds.

If we were to assume that prudence *alone* provides us with good reasons for action, then we would be left with the normative theory called "ethical egoism." This theory tells us that we have reason to promote our own welfare but no reason to promote others' welfare, unless that happens to serve us indirectly. It tells us, in effect, that moral principles are unsound so far as they require us to compromise our own welfare for others' sake. This theory is not nihilistic about values, since it respects some normative judgments. But it leaves no significant room for "other-regarding" values.

Theorists have generally been unwilling to leave matters there. Some, like the English philosopher Thomas Hobbes (1588–1679), have tried to show that moral principles can be derived from or reduced to prudential considerations.[45] Others, such as Joseph Butler (1692–1752), have tried to show that one's personal welfare is so tied up with others' welfare that a policy of prudence, intelligently applied, will lead us to adopt attitudes of concern for others and to act accordingly.[46]

Hobbes's and Butler's theories are compatible with an egoistic ethic, applied with an enlightened understanding of human interactions. Hobbes perceived that we need to restrain ourselves and cooperate with others in order to secure our own private ends, and Butler saw that bonds of affection are needed to enrich our lives. But they represent a tendency to legitimize other-regarding considerations.

The explanation for that tendency may be that egoism fails to offer any clear, general guidance for settling disputes and adjudicating conflicts of interest. If we assume that morality is required at least for such purposes, then we shall seek some principles that transcend the limits of egoism – that deal with such matters from a neutral standpoint. And utilitarianism may be appealing because it seems a reasonable, *neutral* principle for dealing with such problems: when interests conflict, it says, we should serve the greatest aggregate interest. This seems a plausible basis for decision, one that promises each person the best chance for the best result. Utilitarianism may therefore seem a reasonable standard for prudent individuals to adopt in a social setting, on the assumption that each stands to lose if all act egoistically.

But this argument is far from conclusive as it stands. It does not take into account possible conditions in which everyone's interests might be served by some different standard; nor does it consider variations in individual circumstances; so it does not show that all persons at all times would be best served by the adoption of a utilitarian approach to social issues.

But the idea that utilitarianism is a neutral principle suggests a further argument, which does not tie it to the coat-tails of prudence. This may be sketched as follows.[47] The only possible source of value is human interest, which must be understood in terms of desire or preference. Human interest also provides the only rational basis for action. If an existing interest can be served, that creates a reason to do whatever would promote the interest. But values sometimes conflict and decisions among them must be made. The only rational basis for such a choice must be found in human interest itself. Interests can be ordered in terms of the degree of satisfaction or frustration their realization would produce. One accordingly has reason to promote satisfaction to the maximum degree possible.

This argument assumes that the value something *has* is a function simply of the value that we place on it by *desiring* it (directly or indirectly), and that value, so understood, should be promoted as much as possible. These points need closer examination.

Welfare and other values

Utilitarians sometimes claim to respect all basic values and to take the only neutral position with respect to them by urging that all values be promoted as much as possible. But there are at least two ways in which the neutrality of utilitarianism might be challenged. One might claim, first, that utilitarianism is not neutral with respect to how decisions should be made, because it is possible to adjudicate conflicts of interest in principled ways without maximizing welfare. One might claim, secondly, that utilitarianism ignores certain values. Furthermore, one might question whether an individual's desires or preferences always provide a good reason for action – or at least one that is morally relevant.

We can illustrate the first two points by contrasting utilitarianism with a simple form of egalitarianism, which claims that institutions should promote *equal* welfare. This principle does not question the utilitarian definition of individual good, but it claims that such considerations should enter into social decisions in a different way.

In order to contrast utilitarianism with egalitarianism, we must suppose that the interests of different individuals sometimes conflict and cannot simultaneously be satisfied, so that equalizing satisfactions will not maximize them. If decisions must then be made, some will gain, absolutely or relatively, only as others lose. The utilitarian believes that interests should be served as much as possible, without regard to how the benefits and costs happen to be distributed. The egalitarian, by contrast, does not insist that we must maximize overall benefits or minimize overall costs. He is concerned instead with how benefits and costs are distributed.

Suppose a decision must be made concerning a run-down neighborhood in which live people with low incomes and, by and large, low welfare levels. For simplicity's sake we shall assume that any scheme for rehabilitation of the neighborhood would bring benefits to the community, through business profits, construction jobs, and improved housing. Let us also assume that there are two feasible alternatives, one of which must be chosen. The first would improve existing houses in the neighborhood primarily for the benefit of those already living there. The second would replace those houses with more expensive accommodations. Both schemes would benefit both rich and poor, but not in the same way. Let us suppose that the first scheme would benefit the poor more than the rich because it would be less profitable for business interests, but would improve housing for those in greatest need, while the second scheme would benefit the rich more than the poor because it would be more profitable for business interests and would provide more high-rent housing, but would increase crowding and rents in low-income neighborhoods.

The first scheme would tend to equalize welfare. It is quite possible that the second scheme would yield greater net benefits, though these would be unequally distributed. It is possible, in other words, that utilitarianism would favor the second scheme while egalitarianism would favor the first.

The question we now face is whether the utilitarian solution *must* be preferred because utilitarianism is neutral with respect to values. Now, utilitarianism is certainly neutral in the sense that it does not discriminate among the interests that people have. Furthermore, it does not care how benefits and burdens are distributed, so long as net benefits are maximized. Egalitarianism is not neutral in the latter respect, because it cares how benefits and burdens are distributed. It favors equal welfare. It does not do so, however, on the ground that some values are more important than others. It does so because it claims that distribution is itself morally relevant.

Utilitarianism is not just a theory about human good. It is also a theory about how decisions should be made, given a conception of human good. Utilitarianism holds that the welfare of individuals should be maximized. Egalitarianism holds, by contrast, that human welfare should be served, but only within constraints of social and economic equality. Viewed as two theories about how decisions should be made, given a conception of human good, utilitarianism and egalitarianism are on a par: neither is more neutral than the other.

These two theories may be contrasted in a different way. Each represents a *second-order* value, utility favoring the maximization of welfare, equality favoring its equal promotion. Now, utilitarianism holds, in effect, that equality is a value only so far as it promotes human welfare, or only so far as people desire it directly or indirectly. But utilitarians do not generally take this view of the idea that welfare should be maximized. They do not claim that people are generally committed to desiring the promotion of the general welfare. And yet they claim, despite this, and despite the fact that it may not be generally accepted as a basic standard for evaluation, that the principle of utility is a valid standard. Egalitarians can be understood to take a similar position with respect to their own principle.

This suggests that those values which correspond to moral *principles* are not subject to the utilitarian condition, that they be objects of desire. And this is what we should expect. Claims about rights and obligations, for example, as well as the advocacy of social equality, do not presuppose that such values are mere functions of desire. They are held to be standards which are capable, among other things, of adjudicating conflicts of interest and desire.

Before we leave egalitarianism, it may be useful to make one further point about it. Although utilitarianism can claim to be neutral in certain ways, so can egalitarianism. For it can claim to correct for morally irrelevant factors. Consider what utilitarianism might have to say, for example, about the benefits of an unrestricted market. It might hold that prices for goods, including labor, should be determined by the forces of supply and demand because this will maximize benefits on the whole. But the results of such a system are likely to be inegalitarian, with some benefiting considerably more than others. Inequalities result , in part, from conditions over which people have little or no control, such as initial endowments, special needs, and market shortages. Luck plays a major role in such a system. But, an egalitarian might argue, no one begins with a greater claim than anyone else to benefits, and no claim can reasonably be based on happenstance. Given the extensive role of social and historical contingencies in human affairs, the only reasonable mode of social organization would seek to compensate for the morally irrelevant factor of luck by equalizing opportunities for welfare over the life-spans of individuals.

We have seen how it may be argued that utilitarianism is not neutral with respect to values, and, in addition, that it ignores certain values. Let us pursue the latter point further, while also considering whether an individual's desires or preferences always provide good reasons for action.

Utilitarianism holds that the only values that are basically capable of supporting reasons for action are human interests, and that all human interests do so. We have already seen an argument challenging this claim. This is the argument that rape could not be justified, to any degree whatsoever, by the pleasure that it gives a rapist. Many arguments of this type are possible. They seek to show either that some human interests do not provide good reasons for action or that, if they do, they are outweighed by other considerations, such as basic rights.

Let us consider another example. Suppose that Alvin is Bernard's slave. Having grown up under a system of slavery, Bernard is accustomed to the services of his slaves and has become somewhat dependent on them. If Alvin escapes from his bondage or is emancipated, Bernard will suffer accordingly. Some compassion should be shown to Bernard. But does this tend to show that it would be *wrong* for Alvin to escape or to be emancipated? Many would maintain that Bernard's interest in retaining his slaves does not argue for their continued exploitation. It fails to provide a good reason for continuing slavery. Bernard's needs may provide reasons for action, but within moral constraints that prohibit chattel slavery. Suppose, for example, that it would be more costly overall to eliminate slavery and at the same time meet the needs of former slaveholders, such as Bernard, than it would be to continue slavery. Utilitarianism must then argue that it would be better to continue slavery; but the other course of action appears morally preferable.

A utilitarian might argue that slavery could not be supported by utilitarian calculations. He might claim that the burdens imposed on slaves always outweigh the benefits realized by slavery. This is a plausible contention. But a critic would reply that it is beside the point. Whether or not slavery creates more burdens for the slaves, or creates more benefits than could be achieved by any alternative system, it is morally objectionable. It subjugates some people to others' control. It violates their rights.

Rights and obligations

Although human welfare plays a major role in thinking about the way social decisions should be made, other concepts are no less frequently applied. Many legal and moral issues are framed in terms of rights and obligations. We can gain a better understanding of utilitarianism and of moral appraisal generally if we consider how they relate to obligations and rights.

While the concepts of a right and of an obligation are at home within the law, they are also used to describe moral relations that are independent of the law. Consider the example of promising, which is understood to generate rights and obligations. It is generally accepted that one should be true to one's word, and utilitarians typically agree. But they can do so only to the extent that they believe that keeping promises serves the general welfare. And promise-keeping does not always do that. Some critics have argued that the obligation to keep one's promises is more stringent than a utilitarian can possibly appreciate. They believe, in other words, that a utilitarian is committed to breaking promises or to approving others breaking their promises when welfare is thereby promoted, though promises ought in fairness to be kept.

When a utilitarian believes that promises ought to be kept, he has in mind reasons like the following. First, breaking a promise often has direct adverse effects on human welfare. It typically frustrates the desires or preferences of the promisee, who may have acted in reliance on its being performed. Second, promise-breaking may undermine confidence in cooperative arrangements and may discourage individuals from doing useful things that would be risky or impossible without others' assistance. Critics of utilitarianism are aware of these important considerations. To clarify matters, they present examples in which such factors are not present, though the promises seem no less morally binding.

Suppose, for example, that Barbara has made a significant personal sacrifice in order to help Alice, who, while Barbara is dying, promises to provide for the education of Barbara's orphaned children. The promise is made in secret, no one but Alice knows about it, no living person's plans will be upset, and confidence in promises will not be affected by its being broken. From a utilitarian point of view, it seems that Alice should keep her promise to Barbara if, and only if, doing so would best serve the general welfare. If she can produce greater benefits by breaking it than by keeping it, she should break it, even if those benefits do not accrue to Barbara's children but in fact they suffer as a consequence. Critics claim that Alice has an obligation to keep her promise, which means that it would be wrong for her to break it, save for special reasons, and that she is not morally free to break it just because the general welfare could be better served by breaking it. One charge against utilitarianism is thus that it fails to take obligations seriously.

Promises create obligations that arise only by the promisor's own voluntary action. It is commonly thought that we have other obligations, such as the obligation to help others in need, which do not depend on any voluntary act of the individual. It is useful, however, to consider obligations that depend on promises because they are the most difficult to deny. That is because the generally understood point of making a promise is to put oneself under an obligation.

Such an act appears to have the following consequence. If the promisor gives her word freely and without being tricked, she acquires an obligation to perform as she has promised. This obligation, like most others, is not regarded as "absolute" – as requiring one to behave in certain ways without fail, regardless of the circumstances or the consequences of doing so. Obligations can often be overridden, for example, in order to prevent grave dangers to individuals. But, from the fact that one is under an obligation, it follows that one acts wrongly and wrongs another person if one fails to act as the obligation requires, unless some special justification unexpectedly arises. And, from the fact that one can do more good by failing to meet the obligation than by meeting it, it does not follow that one is justified in failing to meet it. The obligation created by promising, for example, is not overridden merely by the fact that one can promote welfare to a greater degree by breaking it than by keeping it. Our example was meant to illustrate these points and to suggest how utilitarianism fails to take obligations seriously.

Critics also argue that utilitarians are unable to take rights seriously either. This point is worth separate treatment, though it is closely related to that of obligation. While the idea that one has obligations seems uncontroversial, the idea that one has rights sometimes generates skepticism. A few brief comments on the concepts of rights and obligations therefore seem in order.

When we use the term "obligation" most broadly, it refers to some standard of behavior, breach of which is wrong, at least in the absence of some overriding consideration. Used more narrowly, however, it concerns something that one *owes* to one or more other persons. In either case, it has implications for the evaluation of one's behavior; in the latter case, however, it also implies that some other person or persons have corresponding rights. Indeed, the idea of having *such* a right seems *equivalent* to the idea that another person has an obligation, so that what having a right amounts to can be inferred from what it is for another person to be under a corresponding obligation, and vice versa. Suppose that I have carelessly damaged your typewriter, which I had borrowed from you. In such a case, you have a right to the return of the typewriter in its original condition (with allowance for predictable wear and tear), so that I am under an obligation to return it to you in that condition, which means that it is my responsibility to repair the damage (or to compensate you for it). Your having a right, however, implies that my behaving as my corresponding obligation requires would not amount to anything like charity or generosity, for it concerns something that is owed to you. Your attitude should be correspondingly different from that of someone who may benefit from my benevolence. What is yours as a matter of right is something you can legitimately claim; it is not something which you must merely hope for or accept with gratitude.

What this suggests is that any mystery that seems to becloud rights can best be dispelled by considering the specific differences it makes to suppose one has a particular right. These differences concern, in part, the appraisal of behavior; but they also involve the attitudes that are appropriately taken by individuals to others.

There are various kinds of rights, and we cannot consider all of them here. But we might single out for special mention one's right to act in a certain way, for in many contexts this has implications about one's own as well as others' behavior. Consider, for example, the idea that one has a right to speak his mind publicly on political matters. This right seems to imply, first, that one may rightfully speak his mind publicly on political matters, in ways or circumstances in which one could not rightfully do so without the right; and, secondly, that others may not interfere with such behavior, at least in some ways or circumstances that might otherwise be justifiable.

The right of free speech, like most rights, is not absolute; it can be overridden in special circumstances. From a moral as well as from a legal point of view, there are cases in which public speech may justifiably be limited. One's soapbox, for example, might be placed before a hydrant to which access may suddenly be needed by firemen. But, if the right of free speech is to be taken seriously, exceptions must be narrowly defined.

According to utilitarianism, public speech may justifiably be limited whenever the net benefits of doing so are likely to be greater than the net benefits of protecting speech. But to reason in this way ignores the right, since the right then makes no difference to the calculations. That is an especially unfortunate mode of reasoning in court decisions, since it should make a difference that Americans have the First Amendment. When courts decide free speech cases, as they sometimes do, merely by "balancing" conflicting interests that exist whether or not the right is established, they in effect ignore the right.

To the charge that they fail to take rights seriously, utilitarians may reply as follows. Experience shows that people are much better off in the long run if a right such as free speech is established and protected by the government. Once it is established, officials have an obligation to protect it. It is useful, from the standpoint of the general welfare, to establish and enforce some rights.

There is force to this reply, since institutions that are justifiable from a utilitarian perspective would most likely establish and enforce some rights. But the utilitarian reply is nevertheless unsatisfactory, for two distinct reasons.

In the first place, while it is plausible to maintain that a public official is under an obligation to discharge the public trust she has accepted, which includes respecting established rights, no such obligation automatically flows from a utilitarian approach to decision-making. A utilitarian official is bound by her theory to permit interference with the exercise of a right whenever the general welfare would be served by such a course of action. She would no doubt often respect rights that ought to be respected, but she would also accept arguments for infringing rights that ought not to be accepted. An implication of the right of free speech, for example, is that speech should be protected *even when* the net cost of doing so (such as the cost of providing police protection for unpopular speakers) is greater than the net cost of denying it. But a utilitarian cannot accept this.

In the second place, while it may be true that people are better off in the long run if such a right is established and protected, this way of looking at the issue ignores other possible reasons for having and respecting legal rights. It ignores the idea that the individual has an *independent* moral right to speak his mind on political matters – a right that may or may not be acknowledged by the law – and that a government *wrongs* those whose speech it limits in order to promote welfare. In a similar way, it ignores the idea that certain institutions, such as slavery, may be unjustifiable because they violate the rights that people have independently of the law.

Principles of justice

The criticisms of utilitarianism that we have sketched involve two important notions: equality and rights. When assumed to be independent of utilitarianism, these are usually treated as considerations of justice.

Justice may be conceived in a wide or a narrow sense. In its wide sense, it represents an overall judgment of moral appraisal. Utilitarianism can be understood as a theory of justice in this sense, one that makes all moral appraisal subordinate to the service of welfare. But we also use the idea of justice to refer to a specific virtue of actions, individuals, and institutions. In this narrow sense, justice is distinguished, for example, from mercy and benevolence.

Utilitarianism has no clear theory of justice in the narrow sense, and utilitarians have generally neglected this aspect of morality. Some utilitarians have suggested that the specific virtue of justice amounts to decisions made uniformly or according to rule. This is plausible when justice concerns the application of rules to particular cases, but it does not seem an adequate conception of the justice of rules themselves or of social institutions more generally.

A traditional approach to justice in the distribution of goods, derived from the Greek philosopher Aristotle (384–322 BC),[48] maintains that goods should be distributed to individuals on the basis of their relative claims. This idea provides no single theory but rather a framework for comparing different conceptions of social justice. Thus one might hold that A and B should receive goods proportioned to their relative degrees of moral virtue, their contribution to the social pool of goods, their respective needs, and so on. Egalitarianism (as we have understood it so far) can then be seen as a theory of distributive justice which maintains that each person has an equal basis for claiming a share of goods. This approach leaves fundamental questions unanswered, such as what goods are properly subject to distribution and how to decide the proper basis for distribution.

A plausible account of justice was suggested by the English philosopher John Stuart Mill (1806–79), who held that moral conduct consists in respecting moral obligations. Since some but not all moral obligations correlate with moral rights, matters of justice represent a special class of moral problems; justice consists in respecting other individuals' moral rights.[49]

Unlike his utilitarian predecessor Bentham, Mill accepted the idea that people have rights that are independent of social recognition and enforcement. Law does not merely create rights, but is expected to respect rights and is unjust when it fails to do so. Bentham scorned this idea, expressed in terms of "natural rights."[50] As a utilitarian, he held that law should serve the general welfare, while the doctrine of natural rights implies that law can be evaluated in nonutilitarian terms.

Skepticism about "natural rights" has often turned on the claim (made, for example, of a right to life, liberty, and the pursuit of happiness) that they are "self-evident." Claims of "self-evidence" in moral matters seem to presuppose some special faculty that delivers moral knowledge and this, as we have noted, has never received adequate defense or explanation. The claim that we have natural rights in its traditional form is thus quite easily discredited.

But the idea is then too quickly dismissed. The idea that people have natural rights can be understood apart from dubious ideas about "self-evidence." At the minimum, the idea seems to be that *every single person* has some moral rights which are independent of special circumstances, agreements, and relationships. The sense of such a claim depends primarily, then, on that of a moral right. And this seems to be the idea of a right that does not depend for its existence (as legal rights seem to do) on some sort of social recognition or enforcement. This idea seems to make as much (or as little) sense as that of a moral principle which is independent of social recognition or enforcement – in other words, a moral standard that may be *discovered* and is not merely imagined or made. In this respect, the idea of a moral right makes as much (or as little) sense as the notion that law should serve the general welfare. It claims that there are grounds independent of law for evaluating legal institutions, policies, and decisions. The idea of a moral right simply does not assume (as utilitarianism does) that those grounds are exhausted by welfare-maximizing considerations.

Mill tried to reconcile the idea of moral rights with utilitarianism by claiming that the principles of justice (understood by him as principles about moral rights) can be defended on utilitarian grounds. But, for reasons we have noted, his efforts seemed bound for failure. It is unclear that utilitarians are prepared to respect rights when their infringement would better serve the general welfare. If so, it is unclear how seriously they can take the idea of rights. In order to respect and thus to accept rights, they would have to limit or qualify their utilitarianism.

Thus, those who reject a purely utilitarian approach to the evaluation of law, and of social institutions generally, typically embrace some notion of justice expressed in terms of moral rights or principles of distribution. Views of these types differ widely; many different fundamental rights have been endorsed, as well as many different bases for distribution. As Mill perceived, we need some way to make systematic sense of these assorted moral notions. Most important, we need a way of defending principles of justice.

Some progress has been made along these lines in recent years. In *A Theory of Justice*, John Rawls developed a comprehensive alternative to the influential utilitarian tradition, including a theory about how principles of justice could be compared and a specific conception of justice defended.[51] We shall devote the remainder of this chapter to Rawls's theories. First, we shall examine the principles that Rawls defends and see how they diverge from utilitarianism. We then discuss Rawls's strategy for defending basic principles.

Rawls's theory concerns justice in the narrow sense, which

he regards as the most important moral test for social institutions: social arrangements are not morally defensible unless they are just. The basic idea of justice, according to Rawls, is the absence of arbitrary inequalities. A set of social institutions is unlikely to treat all individuals alike. It creates distinct social roles and occupations, to which are attached differing opportunities, resources, and burdens. The question for a theory of justice is, what differences may be tolerated from a moral point of view? Rawls's principles concern the "basic structure" of a society[52] – those political, economic, and social arrangements, such as its systems of property and exchange, its form of governance, and its class structure, which determine the fundamental conditions under which people live and their long-term prospects.

Rawls defends two principles of justice, one concerning basic civil rights, the other social and economic inequalities. According to the Equal Maximum Liberty Principle, each person has "an equal right to the most extensive basic liberty compatible with a similar liberty for others." This is understood to cover freedom of speech and assembly, the right to vote and to be eligible for public office, liberty of conscience and freedom of thought, freedom of the person and the right to hold personal property, freedom from arbitrary arrest and seizure. The second principle asserts that "social and economic inequalities are to be arranged so that they are both (*a*) reasonably expected to be to everyone's advantage [also called the "difference principle"], and (*b*) attached to positions and offices open to all [the "fair equality of opportunity principle"]."[53] Rawls thus defends a qualified or limited egalitarianism.

The main features that distinguish Rawls's theory from utilitarianism correspond to respects in which utilitarianism is often thought to be deficient as a comprehensive political philosophy. Consider the matter of social and economic equality. Many utilitarians have argued for equalizing the distribution of goods, because shifting goods from those better off to those who are worse off can usually help the latter more than it hurts the former and can therefore be expected to yield net benefits. But utilitarians have no fundamental objections to inequalities. They are committed to approving social arrangements in which some benefit at others' expense, provided the benefits exceed the costs and the outcome is the highest aggregate welfare level that can be achieved. This is thought by many to be unjust and is condemned by Rawls's difference principle.

Utilitarians have also defended social liberty and political rights, but their allegiance to those values has an uncertain relation to their basic principle. At bottom, utilitarianism has no objection to limiting liberty, distributing it unequally, or restricting political rights, provided that such policies would secure greater welfare. Rawls's first principle implies that we have some rights which any system of social organization must respect. Rights of citizenship and political participation may not be sacrificed in order to increase the aggregate welfare level.

Rawls's definition of benefits also differs from utilitarianism. Utilitarianism is concerned with welfare, understood in terms of pleasure and pain or the satisfaction and frustration of desires or preferences. Rawls defines benefits in terms of "primary goods"[54] – socially distributable goods, such as income and wealth, liberty and opportunity, which need not be considered desirable in themselves, but enable a person to serve her own interests and aims as she chooses. This is meant to provide a publicly ascertainable measure of benefit and to avoid problems concerning interpersonal comparisons of welfare. Furthermore, by measuring benefits in such terms, Rawls commits his theory to some measure of respect for individual autonomy, because the theory does not say how primary goods should be used by individuals. It assumes, in effect, that individuals have a basic right to use such resources as they see fit, so long as they do not undermine just institutions. This fits nicely with Rawls's concentration on the basic structure of society. The principles of justice are meant to regulate the effects of basic institutions and do not apply to private arrangements and transactions. This leaves people free to develop their own associations and additional institutions, provided that they do not undermine the basic structure in a just society. Rawls's principles do not require a specific pattern of distribution for all distributable goods. They are designed to provide a just framework in which individuals can work out further problems and pursue their private or public interests as they choose.

Other political theories, such as utilitarianism, could be developed in terms of primary goods instead of welfare. This would be useful for egalitarian theories in particular, which otherwise face serious difficulties. Individuals differ, for example, with respect to how prudently or wastefully they utilize the resources they secure. If egalitarianism mandates that the actual welfare level of individuals be the same, then it will prescribe periodic transfers from the prudent to the wasteful in order to preserve equality of welfare, which may strike one as unfair. That difficulty would be avoided if egalitarianism were understood as requiring not equal welfare but an equal periodic distribution of some, but not all, primary goods. The result would not conflict with the traditional concerns of egalitarianism.

To understand further the Rawlsian theory of justice and its differences from utilitarianism, we must take as our reference point a particular society with an egalitarian basic structure, measured, of course, by primary goods. If its basic institutions provide for different social roles, the benefits attaching to each must be the same, in the sense that the average person in each social role can reasonably be expected to receive the same net share of primary goods over the course of her life as the average person in any position.

We can also imagine basic institutions for the same society which distribute benefits unequally. In one type of inegalitarian system, the average individuals in some social roles benefit *more* than they would under egalitarian institutions, while others benefit *less*. This type of inegalitarian system involves social trade-offs. In another type of inegalitarian system, the average person in *each* social role is better off than she would be under an egalitarian system for the same society. This type of inegalitarian system involves *no* social trade-offs: no one gains at others' expense. Rawls's difference principle prohibits social trade-offs that flow from the basic structure of society. It condemns the first type of inegalitarian system but approves the second. Inequalities must improve everyone's prospects.

Suppose, for example, that society A has a rigid class structure with limited social mobility. A child assumes the social role and occupation of her parents. Let us suppose that this system involves social trade-offs: some classes benefit more and some benefit less than they would under an egalitarian set of institutions that might be established in the same society. Rawls regards such a system as unjust because those who are worse off do not benefit from the basic inequalities. But such a system might be acceptable to utilitarianism. Under some conditions, systems involving social trade-offs are "efficient" from a utilitarian standpoint: the net benefits (relative to egalitarian arrangements) enjoyed by those entrenched in the upper classes can exceed the net losses for those in the lower classes, so that the aggregated benefits are greater than they would be under an egalitarian regime.

Contrast this case with society B, which includes a social division of labor that makes everyone better off than they would be under an egalitarian regime, though the benefits attaching to different social roles and occupations are unequal. This might happen, for example, if there are unattractive but important tasks, such as coal-mining or garbage collection, which people are not inclined to perform without special incentives, such as higher wages. The result of attaching premium wages to these jobs might be that everyone is better off because the jobs are filled and the important tasks performed, which would not happen otherwise. Though everyone is better off, those who fill those jobs benefit to a greater degree because they receive a larger share of primary goods. Though such a system is not egalitarian, Rawls regards it as just because everyone is better off than they would be under egalitarian institutions for that society. Such inequalities are not arbitrary because they purchase benefits *for all*.

Such a system might be "efficient" from a utilitarian point of view, because it might promote average or aggregate welfare to the maximum degree possible. But a utilitarian might also reject such a system, if there were some alternative system that promoted welfare to a greater degree.

Neither utilitarianism nor Rawls's theory automatically condones existing social arrangements. We live in societies with great social, economic, and political inequalities. Some may argue that current arrangements promote welfare to the maximum degree possible, and thus that they can be defended on utilitarian grounds. But that is doubtful. The system of social transfers sometimes referred to as "the welfare state" suggests how equalization can raise the average welfare level. It is likely that welfare could be more effectively promoted by more radical social surgery than contemporary political leaders are prepared to contemplate. If so, our system could not be justified on utilitarian grounds.

Some may argue that the inequalities within our system can be justified under Rawlsian principles because everyone is better off than they would be under egalitarian arrangements. But that is even more doubtful. The occupants of some social positions receive enormous shares of primary goods without performing any useful social functions at all. And, while some of the special benefits enjoyed by those in the highly paid professions, such as law and medicine, may be needed to attract competent individuals to those jobs, it is arguable that the benefits actually received exceed the level required to insure that those tasks are performed well. Such inequalities as these that flow from basic institutions could not be justified under the difference principle. Our system also seems to require that there be a permanent pool of unemployed as well as low-paid laborers, and individuals within these groups may well be worse off than they would be under egalitarian arrangements. That too would violate the difference principle.

One of the most important primary goods recognized by Rawls is something we would not ordinarily think of as a socially distributed good, namely self-respect – a sense of one's own worth and the worth of one's aims, goals, and plans. To experience a minimally decent and acceptable existence, one must think oneself and one's own concerns to be worth something. It is argued that economic and social advantages, such as income and wealth, cannot compensate for the lack of self-respect. Self-respect becomes an issue for social justice in the following way. Our attitudes toward ourselves are affected by others' attitudes toward us. The development of self-respect by and large requires a generally shared belief that each person has the same basic rights, that each should be free to chart her own course in life, and that each is qualified to participate in the governance of the community. Self-respect, and thus the basic good of the individual, can only be served if institutions reinforce such attitudes. Rawls argues, therefore, that justice requires that certain basic rights and liberties be maximized and distributed equally and that the various roles in society should be open to all.

Establishing a formal system of equal basic rights and liberties when people are starving might amount, of course, to an empty gesture. In that case, social resources should be marshaled to establish more favorable conditions, in which ordinary citizens can effectively exercise the rights and liberties of citizenship. Under conditions such as we live in today, when no one should have to struggle for subsistence, benefits should be distributed so as to permit the effective exercise of equal basic rights and liberties.

The two principles of justice developed by Rawls thus represent a "special conception" of justice, which applies to those societies that are capable of generating sufficient goods to make political participation a real alternative for individuals and civil rights practically meaningful. In other conditions, covered by the "general conception" of justice, liberty may be limited, but only as part of a general program of promoting conditions that are favorable to the effective exercise of basic rights and liberties. Once those conditions are realized, the special conception of justice comes into effect.[55]

Rawls's theory of justice may be summarized as follows. Social justice requires first and foremost that the basic structure of society not incorporate any arbitrary inequalities, as measured by the goods that people by and large require to serve their own interests and secure their own ends. Inequalities are arbitrary unless they can be expected to make the average individual in each social role better off than she would be under an egalitarian regime. This represents a compromise – a kind of reciprocity – between those who might secure greater benefits under a utilitarian regime and those who would then do worse and might therefore insist upon complete equality instead. When social resources are sufficient to provide conditions that favor the effective exercise of political rights and liberties, then equal rights and liberties should be established for all.

Justice as fairness

Rawls defends these principles in two closely related ways. He maintains that they conform to and account for our most considered judgments about social justice, and he develops a "social contract" argument for them. We will concentrate on the latter argument, because it represents an important political tradition which we have not previously acknowledged.

Rawls claims that his principles are those that "free and rational persons concerned to further their own interests would accept in an initial position of equality as defining the terms of their association."[56] Rawls's argument relies on considerations of prudence regulated by minimal assumptions about the character of moral reasoning.

Social contract arguments are commonplace within political theory, but Rawls's contract argument is different from those with which we are most familiar. Contract arguments usually seem to claim that we or our ancestors have been parties to an agreement that establishes a political structure or commits us to obedience. They seek to show why one is under an obligation to abide by the laws of one's society. Such arguments are exceedingly dubious. Many who are supposed to be bound by the alleged agreement have no recollection of making one, and it remains a mystery how an agreement entered into by others could bind those who are not parties to it. Attempts to assuage such doubts may suggest, first, that the agreement is merely "hypothetical" – something it would be reasonable for one to make – but then it is unclear how one could be bound by an agreement that one has never made. Other defenses of the usual social contract arguments transform them completely, into arguments based, say, on the idea that it is *unfair* not to obey the laws of one's community when one has received benefits resulting from others' obedience and one remains within the community. The notion of a contract is replaced by distinctly different moral reasons for obeying the law

Rawls's version of the contract argument neither assumes that individuals have made a pact nor concerns the formation of society or obedience to its laws or current rulers. The argument is intended to show that certain moral principles are binding on us, because they would be accepted by prudent individuals under special conditions which bear a significant relation to our own circumstances.

In ordinary social life we find that our interests clash with those of others, but that we are capable of making ourselves better off through cooperative arrangements. We need to determine a mutually acceptable basis for restraint and cooperation. We will not discover this through the use of pure reason or natural science. It does not follow, however, that principles are entirely arbitrary – that nothing soundly can be said either for or against any principles. Rawls's contract argument is intended to show how principles can be evaluated.

We can identify mutually acceptable principles by applying minimal ideas about morality to our situation. We seek *general* principles, which apply to all relevant cases and are not tailored to benefit special interests. We also need a *fair procedure* for selecting them – one that regards each person as fundamentally free and deserving of consideration equally with others. Fairness helps determine a procedure that enables us to compare alternative conceptions of justice.

We sometimes have occasion to design procedures that are intended to serve a predetermined end or to achieve a predetermined result. Assuming that the criminal code is just, for example, we wish a criminal trial to insure that those who are guilty will be convicted but that the innocent will be acquitted. Viewed in this light, a procedure that insures such results may be considered just. Criminal procedures are imperfect, however, so the best we can hope for is "imperfect" procedural justice. In other cases, we may be able to design procedures that guarantee a predetermined result; then we can achieve "perfect" procedural justice. Suppose, for example, that a pie must be divided equally among several people. If we assume that each person wishes as big a slice as possible for himself, then we can have it distributed as it should be if the person who divides it knows in advance that he will take the last slice left after others have chosen theirs. He can make sure that he will get as big a slice as possible only by dividing the pie equally.

The sort of procedure we require is an instance of neither perfect nor imperfect procedural justice but rather of "pure" procedural justice. We do not begin with a fixed idea of the correct outcome. Rather, the fairness of the procedure makes the outcome fair, as in the case of a well-designed lottery. The outcome will be just *only because* it flows from a fair procedure. Suppose, for example, that our city faces an epidemic of a dangerous infectious disease against which people can be protected by a serum that is available in limited quantities. There is not enough to go around. Let us assume that each person has as much of a claim as any other to receive the protective inoculation. We know that some can be protected, but we have no basis for deciding who they should be – none, save for recourse to a fair procedure, such as a lottery, which gives each person an equal chance to secure the needed dosage.

If principles of justice are not to be found in pure reason or nature, we must begin our inquiry without any independently certifiable basis for deciding how goods should be distributed or conflicting claims adjudicated. The procedure that we are seeking can therefore be a matter for neither perfect nor imperfect procedural justice. It must be a matter for pure procedural justice. If we can design a fair procedure for arriving at universal agreement, the outcome of the procedure – a set of principles – will be just, and decisions following them will be just too. The application of the principles to problems of social distribution will be just insofar as it yields decisions that depend entirely on a fair procedure. This is the idea of "justice as fairness."[57]

A fair procedure for this purpose is, then, an attempt by free and rational individuals, who cannot exercise any coercive power over the others, to determine mutually acceptable ground rules for their basic institutions by deliberating in an unbiased way, undeflected by considerations of special interest. This is an ideal that we can at best approximate. But the ideal makes sense, as we are capable of recognizing cases in which the ideal is not satisfied. For the purpose of determining what the ideal implies, Rawls develops his contract argument. He describes a situation in which the ideal is satisfied. He imagines, for example, that a group of individuals are subject to a "veil of ignorance" which prevents them from remembering specific facts about themselves and their conditions, so that they are incapable of skewing principles to serve their own or other special interests. This corresponds to the idea that, in our deliberations concerning principles, we must reason impartially and must not be deflected from mutually agreeable principles by considerations of special interest. Rawls also imagines that the parties to the contract have a full understanding of psychology and social dynamics, so that they can appreciate how competing principles would work out in practice. This corresponds to the idea that such decisions should be informed by facts about the human condition and can be corrected on the basis of increased understanding.

The parties to the imaginary contract do not use moral reasoning. They do not seek a compromise between differing moral positions. Rather, moral notions enter into the contract argument by suggesting constraints on prudential reasoning (it must not be skewed to serve special interests, for example) and on the results (which must be general principles, applying to all societies).

So the contract argument is designed to show what any group of individuals would agree to, on prudential grounds, when their reasoning is limited by minimal moral constraints, such as the idea of impartiality, and is informed by an understanding of the interests at stake. We are not perfectly prudent, and we accept the idea that prudential judgments are corrigible. In a similar way, we are not perfectly impartial but, if we make the most minimal moral assumptions, then we are committed, Rawls believes, to accepting such constraints as impartiality. For these reasons, the contract argument is supposed to certify principles that we are deeply committed to accepting. In this sense, those principles – *whatever* they may be – are to be regarded as binding on us and on *anyone* who meets those same conditions.

Who could that leave out? It is difficult to imagine anyone to whom prudence is inapplicable. But what about the moral constraints, which are essential to the argument? If these amount to the most minimal assumptions of a morality, then they apply to anyone who wishes to press any claim on others in moral terms. Anyone who adopts a moral point of view is committed to submitting his claims to adjudication under general principles that would be generated by a fair procedure, a procedure capable by its very nature of generating a just result. The argument therefore is inapplicable to an ethical nihilist, who refuses to take any moral values for granted, even the thinnest notion of procedural fairness; but only to a fully consistent nihilist, who rejects morality completely and refuses to consider any issues in moral terms. Such a person cannot believe, for example, that he has any rights or that anyone can wrong him. He is a very special case indeed.

The idea behind the contract argument is theoretically attractive because it purports to show the moral position that one can justifiably take. The argument succeeds, however, only if it can be made to work – only if its moral assumptions can be kept to a bare minimum and it is capable of ranking one set of principles, one conception of social justice, above all others.

Rawls's argument for his own principles can be understood as an application of this general strategy. Rawls claims, for example, that individuals so ideally situated would first of all decide to use the index of primary goods as a public basis for determining benefits. They would then decide to use as their basis for comparison what could be achieved under egalitarian institutions. But they would be prepared to accept inequalities if it were prudent to do so. This leads to one of the more controversial aspects of Rawls's defense of his principles.

If prudent individuals were to adopt the familiar strategy of seeking to "maximize expectable utility," they would then be bound to select a form of utilitarianism for evaluating the basic structure of society. Rawls argues that, given the special conditions of the decision to be made, a "maximin" strategy is preferable. This would insure that those who wind up at the bottom of any social structure fare at least as well as they could fare under egalitarian institutions. (Indeed, Rawls claims that his ideal contractors would wish to make conditions as good as possible for those worst off.) They would be prepared to tolerate only those inequalities flowing from the basic structure of society that benefit all. This reasoning generates Rawls's difference principle. For reasons already suggested, Rawls then argues that such contractors would also require a system of basic rights and liberties which could not be compromised with considerations of welfare, at least under conditions favoring the effective exercise of such rights and liberties.

Three sorts of questions may be raised about this line of reasoning. First, and most fundamentally, does the contract argument provide a general *justification* of moral principles? Second, does Rawls apply the contract strategy *soundly*? That is, does he succeed in showing that his principles would be

chosen in such circumstances and therefore that, if the basic
idea of the contract argument is sound, those principles are
binding on us here and now and should regulate our judgments
of social justice? Third, are Rawlsian principles acceptable
within a broader *coherence* argument? That is, are we
prepared to give up conflicting reflective moral judgments in
favor of his principles? We have said something relevant to the
first question. To answer the second we would have to engage
further in the complex continuing controversy over Rawls's
argument, which would not serve our main purpose here. But
we can add some comments on the third question.

One might wonder whether, as Rawls implies, it is always
just to allow extra benefits for some in order to secure benefits
for others. The idea seems reasonable in the abstract, but we
can imagine situations in which some members of society
threaten to withhold their needed services unless they are given
extra benefits. Imagine, for example, that doctors band
together and refuse to practice unless they are paid exorbitant
fees – fees much greater than are required to attract competent
physicians (but the doctors rigidly control access to medical
practice). It may be prudent to accede to such demands, but it
does not seem as if such a compromise is required by justice.
Rather, the demands themselves appear unjust. Rawls might
respond to this sort of objection, however, by pointing out that
such examples concern specific arrangements that might be
made within a given society, whose basic structure is not at
issue, rather than the design of the basic structure itself.

One might also wonder whether a system is properly
regarded as unjust simply because Rawlsian principles are not
satisfied, even though all members of the society truly accept
and consent to different ground rules for their institutions.
Consent is often not enough to justify actual arrangements, for
consent can result from unfair pressures brought to bear on
individuals. But, if consent is fully free and adequately
informed and it is periodically confirmed as new generations
take their place within society, it would seem capable of
justifying many arrangements that would be rejected by Rawls,

without violating any rights of individuals. For example, a population may decide not to accept inegalitarian arrangements which would benefit all, because they prefer that all receive equal shares of primary goods. If this is possible, then one can also imagine a population that decides it is worth gambling for greater benefits, which can be secured through institutions that a utilitarian would prefer, even though those at the bottom would be worse off than they would be under an egalitarian regime. If all, including those who wind up at the bottom, truly accept these arrangements, it is difficult to see how they could be faulted on moral grounds. The trouble, perhaps, is that it is so very difficult to be sure that agreement in such cases is genuine – that those at the bottom are neither brainwashed nor subtly coerced into accepting conditions that they would reject if given a fair opportunity to do so.

These few comments suggest a complicating feature of Rawls's actual defense of his principles. The contract argument is developed within the framework of a broader coherence argument designed to reconcile the outcome of the contract argument with the judgments about justice we are otherwise prepared to make. Rawls seems to believe this is required, and not optional, because the basic idea of the contract argument is not powerful enough, all by itself, to generate a unique set of principles. The basic idea of the contract argument can be applied in a variety of subtly different ways to generate different principles of social justice. The effect is to compromise the contract argument, to weaken its claim to establish a conception of justice on the basis of minimal assumptions about morality combined with prudential reasoning. It remains to be seen how serious a compromise this is.

As these last remarks suggest, we have been considering issues in moral theory that are unresolved. What this means, I believe, is not that moral theory simply deals with chronically insoluble problems, but rather that understanding in this realm, as in all others, works at and pushes back the frontiers. Utilitarian notions, for example, have been with us, in more or less coherent form, for centuries; but the development of utilitarian theory and systematic appraisal of those notions have accelerated greatly in the relatively recent past. Progress in our understanding of ideas about justice seems no less noteworthy.

Utilitarianism and contrasting principles of justice have been the focus of our discussion in this chapter, because these represent not only long traditions but also contemporary controversies. We have tried not so much to reach a firm position on these matters as to clarify the issues, to explain some central concepts that have occasioned puzzlement, and – most importantly, perhaps – to demonstrate by example that we can reason extensively about fundamental principles.

In the process, we have acquired a basis for discussing more specific moral problems that arise within the context of law, to which we shall now proceed. It should be emphasized, however, as a point about method in moral theory, that our discussions of these problems will not proceed as if we had already established general principles, but can be expected to contribute to our understanding of the leading principles themselves.

5

Legal coercion and moral principle

Even if law is not by its nature coercive, legal systems typically use threats and force to insure compliance with their norms. Our question is how such practices can be justified.

Two general assumptions provide a framework for this discussion: law is morally fallible, and moral judgments are capable of being sound. If law is morally fallible, we cannot assume that legal uses of coercion are justifiable. It is generally agreed that the use of force and coercion normally needs justification. If that is true, it is appropriate to ask for a defense of legal coercion. It may be noted that the idea that coercion requires justification itself assumes that moral judgments are capable of being sound. Otherwise, there could be no sound moral objection to coercion.

Coercion deprives us of the freedom to choose by our own best lights. Its legal use deprives people of other goods as well, such as possessions and even life. No wonder it seems to require justification. But how can such practices be defended?

This question is usually conceived of as the problem of justifying legal punishment. But it is somewhat broader than that may suggest. For the legal use of coercion is not limited to punishments imposed under the criminal law, since it stands behind all legal arrangements that are enforced, including "civil remedies" in other branches of law, such as the law of

145

property, torts, and contracts. The criminal law provides penalties for acts that are officially classified as offenses, and officials are mandated to enforce its rules. In other branches of the law, however, enforcement proceedings must be initiated by someone who wishes to secure his legal rights. Punishment is provided as a last resort, to supplement legal remedies that are made available, such as compensation for damages and judicial orders to carry out the terms of a contract or to cease activities that violate legal rights. If the use of force and coercion requires justification, the entire range of enforcement practices must be justified.

For simplicity's sake, we shall concentrate on justifications offered for legal punishment. We shall begin by considering traditional "retributive" ideas about punishment and then turn to utilitarianism.

Punishment as retribution

The desire for retribution is familiar. We are accustomed to thinking that someone who acts badly deserves bad treatment in return – or at least forfeits some part of his claim to good treatment by others. If someone who is seeking personal gain or is simply careless of others' interests causes injury, we form an unfavorable judgment of that person's character. Such judgments can be triggered, not only when harm is actually done, but also by someone's failure to satisfy minimal standards of decency and consideration for others. And so we may think that a person deserves punishment for negligent acts, and even for bungled attempts to hurt others which cause no actual harm.

Retributive theories of punishment maintain that retributive attitudes can be translated responsibly into practice. They do not celebrate vengeance or call for blind, unreflective revenge. They call for justice – the justice of treating people as they *deserve* to be treated by virtue of their conduct and the attitudes that conduct represents.

One difficulty that we face in evaluating the retributive approach to punishment is that it often seems to be inadequately developed and limited to the recitation of catch-phrases. A brief survey of some retributive suggestions will illustrate this point and the problems that result.

One of the ideas sometimes advanced is that punishment is justified as a means of "restoring the moral balance." This presumably means that a wrongdoer should be deprived of any advantage he secured through his wrongdoing and his victim should be compensated for his loss. A difficulty facing the application of this theory is that it could not clearly justify requiring compensation of a victim by a wrongdoer, unless the original positions of the affected parties could themselves be judged to reflect justice. More important, the aim of restoring a moral balance between wrongdoer and victim is not generally served by systems of *punishment*, which concentrate on making wrongdoers suffer and typically show little concern for compensating victims.

The problem here is, not that our penal practices may need reform, but rather that punishment is precisely the wrong primary means of achieving the end that this theory assumes. Penal law imposes punishments for specific offenses. Remedial law seeks just compensation for victims from those responsible for their losses. If compensation is what we should require, because justice demands it, then we should concentrate our efforts on providing remedies, not penalties. This type of theory therefore does not help us understand how punishment itself, without compensation for victims, might be justified.

A different traditional idea seems more to the point. The *lex talionis*, which demands "an eye for an eye," seems to have clear implications for at least some cases of wrongdoing. One who takes a life should have his own life taken; one who beats another should be beaten in return; and so on. But, once we go beyond a few simple cases like these, the requirements of the formula are either unpalatable, uncertain, or impossible to satisfy. It is unclear, for example, that we would always be justified in treating wrongdoers as they have treated others, since this would mean torturing those who have tortured others and raping those who are guilty of rape. It is unclear how the formula requires us to punish people for acts that cause no actual harm but only create danger or express irresponsible attitudes, as in drunken driving and tax evasion for personal gain. If punishments can be justified in such cases, the formula seems incomplete. And it is unclear that we can possibly treat wrongdoers as they have treated others, when the acts for which they might be punished cannot be duplicated in penalties. How can we follow the formula to determine punishments for those who lie, cheat, defraud, blackmail, or bribe others? So the *lex talionis* does not seem an adequate basis for justifying punishment. It is at best incomplete, and it seems to imply objectionable instructions in some cases.

Another problem facing the *lex talionis* is that it seems unfaithful to some important retributive ideas. Retributive theories are usually understood to say that punishment must be dispensed in accordance with a wrongdoer's deserts. But our judgments of desert are not tied so tightly, as the "eye for an eye" formula is, to overt behavior and the harm that results. We distinguish between harmful behavior, on the one hand, and the blameworthiness of the individual, on the other. To intend harm is one thing; to cause it unintentionally but carelessly is another; to bring about harm by accident or because one's bodily movements are not entirely under one's control is something else again. It is widely believed that a system of punishment should deal with such cases differently, just as it is believed that punishments can be justified even when no harm is done. The *lex talionis* seems to ignore this vital aspect of personal desert.

A more promising retributive approach to punishment is suggested by Kant's moral theory, which takes into account the attitude of the wrongdoer. Kant's theory has the further merit of providing a basis for the requirements violation of which justifies punishment. Retributive theories usually take for granted that punishment may or must be given for wrong-doing, but they typically fail to provide any clear account of the standards that may justifiably be enforced. Kant's theory offers a basis for determining the standards of morally responsible conduct as well as a justification for punishing violations of those standards.

According to Kant,[58] people are not mere cogs in a mechanistic universe, but "rational agents." We understand what we are doing (at least when we can be held responsible for our behavior). Though we do not always articulate them consciously, we act for reasons. We have some ends, purposes, or goals and we conceive of what we are doing in relation to them. To interpret a person's behavior accurately, therefore, is to attribute to that person a "subjective principle" of conduct or a "maxim" of action which represents how that person truly directs his own behavior. These maxims, not overt bodily movements, are the basis for moral judgments of conduct.

Because we are rational agents, Kant maintains, we are committed to "universalizing" the maxims of our actions. We regard them as principles which any rational agent may properly follow. We "legislate" for all humanity; that is, we are committed to regarding our maxims as principles that should become universal laws of human nature. If I see myself as helping another person in need, for example, then the maxim of my action is to help others who are in need, and I am committed to the view that people should generally help others who are in need. By the same token, if I am really taking advantage of another person's helplessness, the maxim of my action is to take advantage of others' helplessness, and I am committed to the view that people may generally take advantage of others' helplessness.

The Kantian theory applies this notion so as to generate principles of duty. My fundamental duty is to act only on maxims that I as a rational agent could "consistently will" to become a universal law of human nature. Kant believed that a rational agent could consistently will some maxims to become universal laws of human nature, but not all. He believed, for example, that I could not consistently will the universalization of the maxim involved in making a false promise – a promise that I have no intention of keeping. If I act on such a maxim, then I act wrongly. Principles of duty thus negate maxims of action that cannot be universalized in this special sense.

The Kantian theory also uses this notion to justify punishment for breaches of duty. If, in acting on a maxim, I am committed to willing that my maxim become a universal law of human nature, then I am committed to the principle that others may treat me as I treat them. If I am prepared to help others, I authorize others to help me. If I am prepared to take advantage of others' helplessness, I authorize others to take advantage of me when I am helpless.

This seems to provide a theoretical rationale for familiar retributive ideas. It explains what lies behind the "eye for an eye" formula, but qualifies it accordingly. It also explains the retributive idea that a wrongdoer "wills his own punishment." In acting well or badly towards others, one is committed to willing that others treat one in similar ways. If one treats others badly, and they reciprocate in kind, then one can be understood to have "brought the punishment on himself."

The Kantian theory of punishment has questionable theoretical underpinnings, but we shall not concentrate on them here. What needs to be seen is the gap between even such a relatively well-developed retributive theory such as Kant's and the justification of legal punishment.

To suggest the magnitude of the problem, let us first consider a different but more familiar notion, that justice is satisfied when the virtuous prosper and the wicked suffer, which we might call cosmic justice. It rests on a theory of cosmic desert: good people deserve to fare well and bad people deserve to fare badly. Such a theory does not translate into prescriptions for punishment of the sort that humans can satisfy, or perhaps any prescriptions for punishment at all. First, the punishments that are imposed by human beings are meted out for specific actions, not for the sake of cosmic justice. And the practice of dispensing punishments for specific acts cannot be relied on to insure that the wicked will eventually suffer according to their cosmic deserts (nor does it begin to insure that the virtuous will prosper). We could not hope to establish a system that dispensed justice according to cosmic deserts. Second, it is not clear that we ought to try. The doctrine of cosmic justice does not explain how anyone can acquire the right to "play God." From the premise that someone deserves to suffer because he is wicked, it does not follow that I or anyone else has the right to impose punishments in order to insure that result. So it is unclear how considerations of cosmic justice could justify acts of punishing, which are part of what must be justified by a normative theory of punishment.

Similar problems face retributive theories of punishment, including Kant's. If these theories are supposed to justify anything like our usual practices of punishing, then they seek to justify the measured allocation of officially authorized punishments in accordance with prescribed procedures. But traditional retributive theories do not begin to address the institutional aspects of legal punishment. Thus, a theory of legal punishment should presumably show how officially authorized penalties may be imposed for wrongdoing, to the exclusion of private retribution. It must provide, in other words, a *differential* justification for punishing acts, reserving it generally for established authorities. But retributive theories generally fail to do this. They give us no idea how one person acquires the right to punish another or, if they do, they give us no idea why the state should have a special role in punishment. They ignore the political context within which legal punishment occurs.

Similar problems face other theories of punishment. It is sometimes suggested, for example, that the legal use of coercion can be justified if private individuals "transfer" to the state the right to punish those who violate their rights.[59] This assumes not only that individuals have rights that are independent of law, but also that they as individuals are morally permitted to protect and enforce those rights by their own private acts. But it is by no means clear that private individuals are morally entitled to use force in order to protect whatever rights they have. If they lack the right to punish, no such general transfer could take place.

If I have a right, another person may have a corresponding obligation. This is true of some rights, and it can be true outside as well as inside of law, as when others have promised me to act in certain ways, owe me compensation for injuries they have done, or have other debts to me. Not all promises are enforceable in a court of law, for example, but they can give rise to rights and obligations that are recognized as binding from a moral point of view. If others fail to respect my rights or threaten to infringe them, I can be justified in complaining, demanding compensation, and acting in other ways that would not ordinarily be warranted. It does not follow, however, that I may use force whenever my rights are threatened or infringed, either to protect them or to secure an appropriate remedy. That would seem to depend on further circumstances, including the importance of the right and what else may be at stake. If so, we cannot assume that I am in a position to authorize others to act on my behalf by enforcing my rights.

One would also expect that state action is more difficult to justify than private enforcement, even when the latter could be justified. State action does not merely substitute for private initiative, since the state claims in such cases to act on behalf of the entire community. It does not merely enforce my rights, but treats the matter as one of public concern. My rights and disputes concerning them are not automatically a matter of public concern in this respect, however, and I cannot make them such just by willing it. Therefore, the question persists, under what conditions a public authority, which *claims* the right to govern the entire community, can *acquire* the moral right to use coercive means.

To justify the legal practice of punishment is to defend the use of penal sanctions to enforce behavioral guidelines. Although punishment is imposed retrospectively, for acts already done (at least in the standard cases), it is authorized beforehand, when standards for conduct are laid down. So, even if retributive theories say that punishment can be justified by reference to what a wrongdoer has done, what they seek to justify is part of a system that includes the establishment of standards concerning future conduct and the legal consequences of compliance. Any theory hoping to justify legal punishment must take this into account.

This is relevant in two ways. First, a theory of legal punishment should presumably limit such justifications, at least normally, to acts that violate established standards. Even if punishment could not be justified except for acts that are wrong in themselves (*mala in se*), that an act is wrong in itself is not usually taken as a *sufficient* justification for legal punishment. Retributivism seems to demand punishment for all moral wrongs, and many would regard this as excessive. Some derelictions do not warrant public intervention, which might violate further rights or be too costly. More important, it is generally assumed that punishment should be restricted to the enforcement of standards that are laid down in advance. The retributive theory of punishment does not seem to acknowledge this restriction on legal punishment, but it gives no reason for regarding it as wrong. It seems to condone the use of *ex post facto* criminal laws.

Second, the retributive theory provides no clear justification for punishing acts that are *not* wrong in themselves, but that *may* be punished because enforcement of the regulations that prohibit such acts is required to serve some reasonable legislative purpose (*mala prohibita*). Legislation governing traffic and economic competition, for example, is not designed exclusively to prevent immoral acts or to give individuals their just deserts, but is aimed at serving some further purposes – perhaps safety and convenience in the former case, efficiency and fairness in the latter. To serve such purposes effectively, coercive measures may be needed. Legal sanctions are believed justified because they are a necessary means of establishing needed practices and enforcing the required regulations. If these regulations can be justified, and if people have an obligation to abide by such rules, then the imposition of punishment under them might accord with moral guilt and desert, but the justification of such punishments would include a non-retributive element. Traffic regulations, for example, are somewhat arbitrary. They do not mirror moral principles. No Kantian argument is available to show that driving on an arbitrarily determined side of the road or stopping at a light of a certain color is a breach of moral duty and thus subject to punishment. We seem to need a more comprehensive theory of legislation to explain how the enforcement of such regulations can be justified.

According to traditional retributive theories, punishment is required by considerations of justice. The *only* good reason for punishing is the guilt of the individual, and the guilty must be punished as they deserve. Our discussion suggests, however, that moral guilt and desert are not the only relevant considerations. Retributive theories appear to fail because they justify too much or too little. If they justify any punishment at all, they seem to justify punishments in too many cases, and by too many people. But it is unclear that they succeed in justifying any punishment at all, especially by legally constituted authorities, because they either do not show why anyone has the right to punish or why the right to punish should be reserved to the state. They also fail to acknowledge some of the reasons that seem to justify coercive legal rules, reasons that accordingly seem to play an essential role in the justification of punishment under those rules.

These comments on traditional retributive ideas should not be taken, however, as disposing of retributive principles concerning punishment. That is because the notion of a "retributive principle," as it is used in moral theory, includes any standard that would not be counted as utilitarian. Some retributive principles which have been proposed would avoid the criticisms we have noted. Many retributivists, for example, would insist that punishment should be restricted to offenses that have been established in advance, and should not be imposed for all moral wrongs. Similarly, retributive principles may be incorporated into a general theory which provides a justification for restrictions on behavior that is not wrong in itself.

We have so far ignored limited retributive principles like

these because it is unclear that they can be said to have any general, underlying rationale, except as placing moral limits on practices that might be condoned by utilitarians. To understand the point of many such principles, we need first to see why utilitarian approaches to punishment may be thought deficient. So we turn next to utilitarian ideas about punishment, after which we shall come back to "retributive" (nonutilitarian) ideas.

Punishment as useful

Our discussion of retributive theories uncovered a number of problems which in turn suggest conditions to be satisfied by a theory seeking to justify the legal use of coercion. An adequate theory will include standards for legislation; it will enable us to decide what legal norms can be justified, at least if they are to be enforced. It will determine when punishments should be laid down for noncompliance and when other legal remedies should be provided instead. It will help us to construct a schedule of punishments for different offenses. And it will imply that official action involving the use of force and coercion may be justifiable even when private action is not.

Even if we begin with the assumption that punishment may be justified for wrongdoing because it is deserved, we cannot allow ourselves the luxury of stopping there. Not all wrongs are made punishable or remediable, and it is arguable that legal intervention should be limited. For punishment is costly – not only the imposition of penalties, but also the establishment and administration of legal machinery to police wrongdoing and to deal with it systematically. Once penalties are authorized for specific acts, everyone is exposed to the risk of suffering legal punishment, for no system of enforcement is completely reliable. We run the risk of punishing unjustly. Furthermore, resources are scarce, and those devoted to enforcing law must be limited by other social needs. We cannot afford to support the number of police and other officials that would be required to insure that laws are always obeyed or that wrongdoers are always punished. Punishment should presumably be reserved for wrongdoing that is sufficiently important to warrant the costs involved in regulation and that is not better dealt with by other, perhaps less costly means, such as private action or civil remedies.

One reason often cited for supporting a system of legal punishment is that it provides a substitute for private vengeance, which can result in protracted feuds and escalating retaliation. We can avoid human suffering as well as much injustice by employing a system that establishes minimal standards for behavior, authoritatively determines relevant facts, sublimates the desire for revenge, mediates disputes, and draws conflict to a close. If this requires the power of enforcement, legal coercion may be justified.

Legal enforcement thus provides a centralized mechanism for dealing with wrongdoing, real or perceived. Once such a mechanism is established, new needs arise. Cooperation is required to make such a system work – ranging from participation in the process as an official, witness, or jury member to economic support of the institution by paying taxes. Burdens must be imposed on individuals, and coercion may be required to extract them, through subpoena powers and enforceable tax laws.

Other sorts of legal action may be thought justified. It may be inefficient or impossible to serve some social needs, especially in large and complex communities, without central-ized decisions and actions. Public safety and health may require rules regulating sewage disposal and pollution, traffic, and the rationing of vital goods in short supply. In many such cases, enforcement may be required to insure the success of the regulations. These arrangements provide so-called "public goods," from which all stand to benefit. The goods are available to each member of the community, whether or not one contributes efforts, goods, or money as required. One may be tempted to reap the benefits without paying the price. Such arrangements can often succeed despite a few "free-loaders," and they must be designed to survive imperfect compliance. But, if everyone who was tempted to free-load found it easy to do so, the arrangements might collapse and the benefits be lost. To prevent this, enforcement may be needed to insure extensive cooperation by making noncompliance unattractive.

All of this suggests that punishment, and legal coercion generally, must be justified, at least partly, on instrumental grounds, as serving purposes beyond the requirements of retributive justice. And this suggests, in turn, the plausibility of a utilitarian approach to punishment, which we must now consider.

Utilitarianism satisfies many of the conditions that we have laid down for a theory of punishment. It was in fact most systematically developed in the eighteenth century as a basis for legal reform, and was presented as a rational ground of coercive legal institutions and for legal punishments in particular. A utilitarian believes that law should serve the interests of people. If punishment can be justified, it must be in such terms.

Punishment is costly – not only by reason of the imposition of penalties in particular cases and the machinery that is required to administer a system of legal punishments, but also because of the establishment of penalties for certain acts, which both limit personal decisions and expose everyone to the risk of punishment. So punishment cannot be justified on utilitarian grounds unless the benefits that it purchases exceed its costs.

The utilitarian approach to punishment thus involves a kind of "cost-benefit analysis" involving "trade-offs." Punishments cannot be justified simply because they are deserved, and the interests of those who may be tempted to break the law, or who actually do so, must be considered on an equal footing with the interests of all others who are affected. Punishments can be justified only if the decisions resulting in predictable costs would produce greater net benefits than any alternative decisions that could be made.

The traditional utilitarian view of punishment is that it can serve as a "deterrent." When punishment is authorized for acts of certain kinds, the threat or risk of punishment can dissuade people from acting in those ways. That is "general" deterrence. When an individual is punished, he may be prevented from performing such acts, or may be persuaded not to repeat them in the future. That is "specific" deterrence. By and large, general deterrence is considered at the legislative stage of decision-making and specific deterrence at the administrative or enforcement stage. The aim, in each case, is to set the punishment at such a level that the net benefits are maximized, counting harms prevented as benefits and taking costs into account. On this view, the justification of punishment depends on the deterrent effects that can reasonably be predicted, plus any other benefits and costs that can reasonably be expected.

The deterrence theory of punishment is sometimes considered outside this context, when it is assumed that punishment simply aims at eradicating undesired conduct. This leads to the objection that utilitarianism endorses punishments that are disproportionate to offenses and sanctions punishments that are excessively severe. If reckless or drunken driving is hard to eradicate, long prison terms or even capital punishment may be required.

Such arguments may rest on misunderstanding. First, the *utilitarian* version of the deterrence theory insists that benefits exceed costs. Its aim is never deterrence as such, but only the efficient, effective, and beneficial use of coercion and penalties. And neither long prison terms nor capital punishment is likely to be the most effective way of regulating reckless or drunken driving. Second, decisions concerning which acts are to be subject to punishment cannot be divorced, on a utilitarian view, from the justification of punishment itself. We do not decide first on acts to be prohibited and then set punishments designed to eradicate them. Since punishment is costly, not every harmful or dangerous act can usefully be subjected to penal sanctions, for the predictable benefits sometimes would not exceed the predictable costs. By the same token, conduct that is *not* harmful in itself can be regulated, if coercive regulations would promote welfare, as traffic laws are supposed to do. Third, whether a punishment "fits the crime" depends, according to this theory, on whether such punishments can be justified in this purely instrumental way. There may be independent grounds for judgments of personal desert (though on a thoroughly utilitarian view these would have to be based on utilitarian calculations), but these have no weight in the utilitarian version of the deterrence theory.

One objection to the deterrence theory is that punishment is an ineffective means of social control. Crime increases year by year despite the threat of punishment, and the recidivism rate – the proportion of repeat offenders – is high. This is because punishment fails to deal with the root causes of crime. The penal system provides punishment for acts of certain types but does not attack the underlying conditions that make people break the law. As a result, it fails to prevent harm as effectively as it should do. For this purpose, some believe, we need therapy rather than punishment. Crime, they say, is a pathological condition. Psychological analysis is needed to identify the specific form of this pathology in each case, and therapy is needed to rehabilitate criminals. Prisons should be replaced by institutions dedicated to the protection of society, in which offenders would be required to undergo treatment until they could safely be returned to life on the outside.

too expensive

Criticisms like these appear to combine a utilitarian approach with disillusionment concerning general deterrence and the conviction that contemporary psychology is equipped to deal with crime. They raise issues of principle as well as fact.

The deterrence theory depends on assumptions about the effects of legal punishment, and these assumptions can be doubted. But some arguments against it are invalid. Recidivism shows that the familiar practices of punishing can fail to change the conduct of those already convicted. This does not show, however, that punishment does not generally deter. For it may well be that many of those who never run afoul of the law *are* deterred by the threat of punishment and would have committed crimes had there been no risk of legal penalties.

The factors determining general deterrence effects are

complex and insufficiently understood. There is evidence that impulsive crimes are least affected by threats of punishment, but less impulsive acts within the same categories (such as homicide) may well be discouraged by the threat of severe penalties. There is evidence that deterrence effects are enhanced more by increasing the likelihood that one who breaks the law will suffer punishment than by increasing the severity of penalties that are authorized without making punishment more probable. This seems true, for example, of laws against drunken driving. While we have limited understanding of these complications, our practices are not uniformly guided by the information we have. There is much resistance to the imposition of penalties for drunken driving, for example, despite evidence that it can be much better controlled by rigorous enforcement.

It should be emphasized, however, that utilitarians want nothing to do with punishment if it does not work. The deterrence theory is not part and parcel of utilitarianism, but is supported by it only given relevant assumptions about human psychology, costs, and benefits. If coercive threats are ineffective or inefficient, or if we simply do not know enough or cannot learn enough to produce a schedule of punishments for various offenses that can reasonably be expected to have the desired effects, utilitarianism cannot justify such measures. This does not mean that a utilitarian would then give up all means of social control. It is therefore important to consider some of the alternatives to punishment that have been proposed, though we cannot assume that these could truly be justified on utilitarian grounds.

One type of proposal concerns changes in our modes of punishing offenders. It is sometimes argued that we use imprisonment excessively and that alternative methods of control, such as probation, are often more effective. If so, since they are cheaper and avoid the many problems associated with imprisonment, they should be acceptable to a utilitarian. Such reforms do not seem controversial in principle, though they may be difficult to achieve in practice.

The more radical proposal, to substitute a system dedicated to therapy for ordinary methods of punishment, requires more careful examination. This proposal seems to rest on questionable assumptions. While many criminal acts may manifest pathological conditions, that is hardly true in all cases. It is doubtful that civil disobedience is pathological or that no healthy person ever breaks the law. (When the law is sufficiently bad, the only healthy reaction may be to subvert it.) Some ordinary crimes are committed for profit, and these might best be controlled by rigorous enforcement. Furthermore, the proposal to substitute therapy for punishment may be misleading. Neither our understanding nor our practice has developed to the point at which we can assume that "cures" can be found for every mental or motivational pathology. There is also reason to believe that some therapeutic procedures cannot be conducted successfully within a coercive environment; but therapy cannot be mandated except within some sort of coercive setting.

For these reasons, it is understandable that proposals to substitute therapy for punishment usually incorporate the requirement of indefinite detention. Detention is required (in places that are not to be called "prisons," but which must keep offenders securely under control) to make sure offenders are subjected to whatever therapeutic methods are appropriate and available. And it *must* be indefinite, not for a determinate period, because there is no telling how long it will take to effect a cure. Indeed, we cannot predict whether any cure is available or will work. And those who are responsible for certifying that their "patients" have been rehabilitated – so that they can be released without risk to others, without the likelihood of breaking the law once more – will hesitate to authorize the release of anyone about whom they have doubts. Once one is committed to such an institution, therefore, one might be required to remain there indefinitely. This is not only expensive, it is exceedingly harsh treatment for those who are detained, who cannot be guaranteed release at any predictable time, and who may never be permitted to return to life on the outside. The penal system with its limited sentences can well seem more humane and just.

If such methods of social control were truly "cost efficient" in utilitarian terms, that would seem to reflect badly on utilitarianism. But we have inadequate reason to suppose that utilitarianism could truly justify the practices that have been described, though they are often put forward with a vaguely utilitarian rationale. (By the same token, it would be unfair to associate those who advocate therapeutic measures, when they are appropriate and effective, with proposals for indefinite detention that make a mockery of therapy.)

One trouble with many proposals for radically revising the penal system is that they seem dedicated singlemindedly to preventing harmful conduct by whatever means may be effective. That is, they do not seem to take into account the costs that a utilitarian would consider relevant – not only the expense, but also the effects on those convicted or otherwise dealt with by the system.

Some criticisms of the penal system and associated proposals seem to avoid these difficulties. Some critics contend that the system as we know it is excessively influenced by retributive ideas – concerned with moral guilt, when it should aim more effectively at preventing harm. They observe that criminal trials are burdened by the need to establish mental or motivational conditions of the criminal when he performed the prohibited act. These are difficult to establish, and an adversarial procedure is held to be an unreliable method for conducting such an investigation. Furthermore, if we are concerned to prevent harm, we should not confine our system of social control to dealing with those who satisfy the accepted criteria of moral guilt. Harm is done not only by deliberate wrongful acts but also by negligence, accident, and the lack of self-control. It is therefore proposed that criminal statutes be rewritten to eliminate reference to mental or motivational conditions. Criminal trials should be replaced by proceedings to determine whether the accused committed the prohibited act, after which experts would determine how best to deal with the offender.

This proposal addresses an important feature of our criminal laws. Many laws imposing penalties for prohibited acts take into account the mental or motivational state of the individual. Some prohibitions concern only acts that are done with relevant motives, such as fraud, bribery, and harassment. One could not break such a law without understanding what he is doing and doing it intentionally. Laws like these could not be rewritten to eliminate reference to the mental or motivational state of the offender. Other prohibitions differentiate between types of intention and the lack of it. Premeditated murder is treated differently from accidental but negligent homicide. This differentiation reflects, however roughly, widely shared ideas about individual responsibility and desert. Punishment is allocated not just for harm done but also on the basis of personal desert.

The proposal we are now considering would eliminate such distinctions. It would substitute a system of "strict liability" for the more familiar criminal statutes. Under many laws, certain conditions either "exculpate" from criminal liability entirely or "mitigate" the degree of liability. These "excusing conditions" include acting in ignorance, under duress, and when one's self-control is significantly impaired. Many believe it only fair to limit criminal liability in such cases. Laws imposing strict liability refuse to do so. They lay down prohibitions specifying punishable acts that can be identified without regard to the mental or motivational condition of the offender. Many traffic regulations are of this type. The proposal under consideration would expand the range of strict liability as far as possible. It would eliminate the legal recognition of excuses and aim at preventing the recurrence of harmful behavior. Under it, convictions would not differentiate between a murderer, one who kills in self-defense, a driver whose car kills a person who runs in front of it, and one who causes another's death when he is temporarily or permanently unable to control his bodily movements. After conviction, *fallible maybe the outcomes would be worse.*

psychological investigation would seek to determine how to deal with each individual, in order to prevent further harmful acts.

Serious difficulties face this proposal. As we have noted, some crimes cannot be defined without reference to intent or motivation. And it is doubtful that we should prefer a system that eliminates distinctions such as those between murder, negligent homicide, and accident. Odium attaches to criminal punishment, and this may well enhance the deterrent effect of criminal prohibitions. Conviction is not merely descriptive of behavior but also condemnatory. If judgments of personal desert can be defended, the condemnatory function of criminal conviction and the distinctions embedded in the legal recognition of excuses can likewise be defended as required by justice. If a strict liability system would eliminate the condemnatory function of conviction, then we would lose both the associated deterrent effects and the symbolic significance of conviction under justifiable laws. If a strict liability system would retain the condemnatory function of conviction, however, it would unjustly condemn some who should be held blameless. That would conflict with and undermine moral distinctions that appear important.

Bentham argued, in effect, that a strict liability system could not be justified on utilitarian grounds.[60] He believed that a useful system would accommodate the generally recognized excusing conditions and respect such moral distinctions, because the threat of punishment could not prevent someone from performing a prohibited act in such cases. Punishments would then have costs without securing any benefits. If a person does not realize what she is doing or is not in control of her bodily movements, for example, then she cannot be deterred by the threat of punishment, so to punish her would be counterproductive.

But Bentham's argument is invalid.[61] At the legislative stage of decision-making, the question for a utilitarian is whether a law imposing strict liability would produce greater benefits than one accommodating excuses. Bentham's answer ignores some deterrent effects of strict liability. Once excusing conditions are permitted to prevent convictions or reduce penalties, it is more difficult to obtain a conviction and, if a conviction is secured, punishment may be less than it would otherwise be. This may be desirable when it affects just those who are the intended beneficiaries of excusing conditions, but others may benefit too. Excusing conditions decrease the risks attached to prohibited acts, either by decreasing the probability of conviction or decreasing the likely penalties. Those who contemplate performing such acts are then encouraged to calculate the chances that they might either escape punishment or minimize it by claiming, if and when they are prosecuted, that they satisfied one of the excusing conditions. And a false claim has some chance of succeeding. So deterrent effects are likely to be reduced by the legal acceptance of excusing conditions. Strict liability might then be justified, on utilitarian grounds, provided the harms prevented by discouraging such deliberate acts are greater than the harms done to those who are punished though they could not help doing what they did.

It is unclear what a utilitarian calculation would yield in such cases – whether strict liability should be condemned or condoned by a consistent utilitarian. It might turn out, ironically, that Bentham was right after all, because the harms resulting from strict liability laws exceed the benefits. But this would not satisfy a critic who believes that excusing conditions must be respected by the criminal law, as a matter of justice, and should not be contingent upon the results of "cost-benefit analysis." He would contend that someone who satisfies an excusing condition is less blameworthy than someone who does not, and thus deserves less punishment or none at all.

With regard to legal excuses, then, the critic of utilitarianism makes the following complex charge. If strict liability is condoned because it is useful, then people will be punished who do not deserve punishment, because they are not blameworthy; or people will be punished more severely than they deserve. But when strict liability is rejected on utilitarian grounds, it is condemned for the wrong reasons. If that is right, then the utilitarian theory of punishment is fundamentally flawed. It may give part of the truth about how to regulate the criminal law, but it could not be considered complete. For, in that case, nonutilitarian principles of desert would have a proper role to play in determining punishments.

A somewhat similar problem arises at the administrative stage. It may be useful to punish someone so as to enhance deterrent effects. Unusually severe, "exemplary" punishments are a case in point. But these involve those who are assumed to have committed a crime, and the more striking problems arise when someone is singled out for punishment though he is not believed guilty. It is argued, for example, that a utilitarian prosecutor would be prepared to frame an innocent person in order to prevent greater harm, as when race riots are imminent and only quick action in response to an interracial crime will prevent violence. In this sort of case, the critic maintains that utilitarianism condones the punishment of innocent persons. When it does not do so, that is for the wrong reasons. Moreover, a person punished in this sort of case not only is morally innocent but is not even guilty of breaking the law.

In response to this argument, it has been suggested that an official would not act in such a way under utilitarian institutions, because he would not be free to calculate the consequences of his conduct but would be required to follow the rules. To adopt a system of punishment is to commit oneself to rules that predicate punishment on past acts. The alternative would be a system that allows officials discretion to frame innocent people when that is likely to secure great benefits. But, it is argued, the adoption of such a system would undermine welfare, because it would make us all liable to such acts by officials and would accordingly decrease our sense of security and our ability to control our own fates.[62]

There are two problems with this answer. First, a utilitarian is committed, not to abiding by rules that a utilitarian legislator would prefer, but to making decisions on utilitarian grounds. If a utilitarian system of punishment limited his choices, he would hesitate to break those rules, for fear of undermining the desired effects of following them. But he would have no stronger commitment to the rules. Utilitarianism can avoid this only by *qualifying* the theory so that it limits utilitarian decisions to the legislative level. But the point of doing this would be that unrestricted utilitarianism is morally objectionable. It would concede the point of the objection. Second, if it is wrong to railroad innocent persons, that is not because it would be counterproductive to do so. The wrong is the injustice done to an innocent person. Even if the utilitarian comes to the right conclusion, he does so for the wrong reasons. Here, as elsewhere, his theory is alleged to give, at most, just part of the truth.

Nonutilitarian principles

According to traditional retributive theories, the usefulness of punishment is morally irrelevant. For reasons suggested earlier, it is difficult to believe that a satisfactory theory of punishment will be thoroughly retributive. But, for reasons suggested in the previous section, it is difficult to believe that a utilitarian theory will be adequate, since it seems to clash with considerations of justice.

Modern "retributive" theories often take the form, therefore, of setting moral limits on the legal use of punishment, without insisting that other factors are irrelevant. It is assumed that coercive measures can be justified on nonretributive grounds. Retributive principles are supposed to provide moral limits within which other purposes can justifiably be served by coercive measures.

Retributive principles may argue for the use of punishment even when the social costs are high. More often, however, retributive principles are used to argue for limiting the use of punishment to cases in which people are believed to deserve such treatment. For example, retributive principles may argue against measures that might otherwise be justified on utilitarian grounds which would involve the punishment of innocent persons. Retributive principles argue against strict liability and for the legal acceptance of excusing conditions. They argue against "vicarious" liability – the practice of punishing people for acts performed by others. They argue against the use of secret or retrospective criminal laws, exemplary punishments, and the use of hostages, however useful such measures might be.

The moral point of retributive principles, so understood, might be explained as follows. Punishment is a method of social control that may be used to secure values which are legitimately served within a just social order. These values are not limited to retributive justice, but might include the service of basic human needs, perhaps the promotion of human welfare more generally, and respect for individuals' rights. The idea of a just social order involves, furthermore, an ideal of the individual. A person is not a cog within a social machine, subject to manipulation or "treatment" by others, but is capable of self-control. Someone capable of self-control is accountable to others and can be held responsible for his behavior. The authorization of punishment for certain acts tells the individual what he must be prepared to "pay" for so acting. If those authorizations can be justified, their imposition can also be justified, by reference to the individual's decision to risk paying the price. But the price may not be exacted unless the individual was in fact capable of making a relevant choice – unless the assumed conditions of self-control were satisfied.

This interpretation of retributive principles as placing moral limits on the use of punishment amounts to the idea that it is *fair* to punish when those principles are satisfied and *unfair* otherwise. It does not simply picture punishment as a penalty for wrongdoing, but sees it, when justifiable, as part of a "fair bargain" between the individual and the rest of the community. The fairness of the bargain is not determined by abstract calculations of the fittingness of the punishment for the crime. The authorization of punishment must be justified, and in many cases this cannot be explained in purely retributive terms. The justification of punishment cannot be complete without a larger normative theory of law, which determines when specific laws can be justified and obedience can legitimately be required. Our discussion suggests that such a theory will be neither purely utilitarian nor bereft of utilitarian considerations. Human welfare is relevant, but it is not the only factor.

Some criticisms of our criminal justice system do not attack punishment as such but concern conditions that might be changed by reforms within the system. Poor people do not have equal access to adequate counsel and, along with members of minority groups, they tend to be given more severe sentences upon conviction. Inordinate delays before trial are especially difficult for those who cannot raise bail. Prison conditions are often brutalizing and promote crime rather than prevent it.

Such criticisms concern aspects of society at large, not just the penal system. Adequate reforms could not be limited to measures affecting only police, courts, and prisons, but would require major changes in the social order. The general problem posed by such criticisms is whether punishment can be justified when the social order is significantly out of joint. We have not addressed this issue. We have merely tried to understand the considerations that lie behind the legal use of punishments under favorable conditions, when not only the laws themselves but their application to particular cases might be justified.

6

Liberty and law

In the last chapter we took for granted that coercion requires justification. Coercion limits liberty, so that protection of liberty under law is closely tied to the problem of legal coercion. But our focus in this chapter is different. Experience shows that law frequently threatens to invade certain areas of choice which many regard as especially important to secure from legal intervention. We shall examine some of the problems posed by legal paternalism, the enforcement of morality, and restrictions on speech, with the aim of understanding why liberty should be protected.

The problem of paternalism

All of the problems we have listed for discussion in this chapter are dealt with by Mill in his classic essay *On Liberty*. Mill there defends

one very simple principle, as entitled to govern absolutely the dealings of society with the individual in the way of compulsion and control, whether the means used be physical force in the form of legal penalties or the moral coercion of public opinion. That principle is that the sole end for which mankind are warranted, individually or collectively, in interfering with the liberty of action of any of their number is self-protection. That the only purpose for which power can be rightfully exercised over any member of a civilized community, against his will, is to prevent harm to others. His own good, either physical or moral, is not a sufficient warrant. He cannot rightfully be compelled to do or forbear because it will be better for him to do so, because it will make him happier, because, in the opinions of others, to do so would be wise or even right.[63]

Mill objects to legal action (as well as social intervention generally) with certain aims or grounds. He rejects, for example, legal paternalism – actions that require a person to promote her own good or that prevent her from harming herself.

Mill makes clear that he does not object to legal action which promotes the good of those whose behavior is restricted, provided that it can be justified solely on the ground that it prevents harm to others. Consider prohibitions on smoking in public places. Mill would condemn such restrictions if they seek to prevent smokers from causing injury to themselves. But if, as is currently believed, one person's smoking can cause injury to others, because it pollutes the air that others breathe, then Mill would entertain prohibitions on smoking, for the sake of others. He would presumably approve of a restriction only when its predictable costs are less than the harm to others it is likely to prevent.

Mill's doctrine of liberty does not square with normal practice. Legislation requiring motorcyclists to wear safety helmets and occupants of automobiles to wear safety belts, for example, seems designed primarily to protect those whose behavior is restricted from the harmful consequences of their own decisions. This is not to say that we always interfere with dangerous activities; mountain climbing is a clear example. If our practice is erratic, this may reflect some uncertainty we have about the justifiability of paternalistic intervention. It gives us all the more reason to see whether anything like Mill's principle of liberty or some alternative to it can be defended.

Objections to paternalism are often couched in terms of rights. It may be held, for example, that one has a right to do whatever one wishes, provided that others' rights are respected, which presumably involves taking care to avoid unnecessarily harming others – a position that amounts to something like Mill's principle of liberty. This is an important idea, to which we shall return. First we must take note that Mill rejects such a defense of the principle of liberty. He does not appeal to fundamental rights. One reason to refrain from doing so may be obvious: the putative right to which one might appeal is roughly equivalent to the principle itself. Unless the right itself could be defended, invoking it in defense of the principle could not prove much. So Mill sets out to defend the principle, which amounts to a defense of the right to do what one wishes, with the qualification that legal interference can be justified for the purpose of preventing harm to others.

Mill claims that the principle of liberty can be defended on utilitarian grounds. He wishes to persuade us that the general welfare would best be served if we limited our reasons for legal interference to the prevention of harm to people other than those whose conduct is restricted. This is a striking claim – first, because it amounts to the defense of an important right by a utilitarian (something which many have thought impossible); secondly, because the utilitarian's commitment to benevolence would seem quite naturally to lead him to condone paternalistic intervention whenever it would promote welfare. If this is true of utilitarians, it is true of anyone who accepts an obligation of benevolent concern toward others. Paternalism is one natural manifestation of benevolence (though of course it might be limited by other moral values). So Mill's utilitarian defense of the principle of liberty, and specifically his utilitarian rejection of paternalistic intervention, are of broad interest.

Mill does not offer a general argument for the principle of liberty. Instead, he marshals arguments for what he takes as its chief corollaries, such as the rejection of legal paternalism. The latter argument may be summarized as follows. Though we are not completely self-centered, we naturally care more about our own interests than the interests of others. For this and other reasons, we know our own interests well, but our knowledge of others' interests is largely limited to generalizations that ignore the special needs and concerns of other persons. We thus have good grounds for judging when others' conduct threatens us, but unreliable grounds for judging the effects of others' actions on their own interests. So the use of coercion for the purpose of "self-protection" can often be justified, but our ignorance of others' interests means that our interference with their conduct for their own sake often does more harm than good.[64]

This is Mill's utilitarian argument against paternalistic intervention. It does not assume that we have a general right to liberty, but rather aims to show that we should treat liberty as a right because we would collectively be better off in the long run if we did so. Mill's argument is not entirely persuasive. For one thing, we are often ignorant of our own interest, or at least of what measures tend to serve or undermine it. Furthermore, we sometimes seem to know enough of other people's interests to put us in a good position to protect them. It would seem that paternalistic intervention can and does pay off in some cases, so that a blanket rejection of it, at least on utilitarian grounds, could not be justified. Despite the initial costs of withdrawal from smoking, for example, there is good reason to believe that its prohibition would do more good than harm in the long run.

To bolster his argument, Mill needs to show that, even though paternalism is sometimes effective, we have to choose between two policies – a policy of allowing paternalistic arguments for social intervention, and a rigid policy of rejecting such arguments. He might reason as follows: we wish to intervene only when that will pay off in the long run, by doing more good than harm, but we cannot reliably enough distinguish in advance those cases in which such interference will pay off from those that will do more harm than good. He needs to show that the only way we can prevent ourselves from doing more harm than good in this area is by refusing to consider intervention on paternalistic grounds. He does not show this, and it is not clearly true.

Furthermore, Mill's argument could not be developed along such lines without undermining utilitarianism and even the principle of liberty as practical guides to action. If paternalism is too risky because we do not know enough of others' interests, then so is most legal action, including the prevention of harm to others. This point may have been obscured to Mill himself by his metaphor of "self-protection," which suggests that, when we restrict conduct in order to prevent harm to others, we do so on the basis of our knowledge of our own interests. But that is a mistake. Most legal action which aims to prevent harm to people other than those whose conduct is restricted is not designed just to protect those who take such action; it is aimed at preventing harm to third parties. In order to justify intervention under the principle of liberty, we must have reliable knowledge of third parties' interests, the interests of people other than ourselves. If, as Mill's argument against paternalism assumes, we lack reliable knowledge of others' interests, then we do not know enough to justify intervention aimed at preventing harm to anyone other than ourselves. On Mill's assumptions, therefore, most legal action designed to prevent people from harming others would be unjustifiable. By the same token, we would be incapable of forming reliable judgments about the general welfare. So the principle of liberty and the principle of utility would both be useless guides to action.

Mill's argument is paradoxical in another way. It rests on the assumption that we know enough about how people have been affected by past actions to conclude that their interests have been adversely affected by past attempts at paternalistic intervention. This suggests that we do have substantial knowledge of others' interests, and it seems to conflict with the idea that we do not know others' interests well enough to determine when paternalistic intervention can be justified.

All of this suggests that a utilitarian argument against paternalism must be severely qualified. And other aspects of Mill's position, as developed in his essays *Utilitarianism* and *On Liberty*, suggest how we might proceed. Mill assumes that we know enough of other people's interests to justify *some* legal actions designed to prevent people from harming others. This suggests that we have knowledge of some interests that people have, even if we are ignorant of others. One possibility worth considering is that people are similar in some important ways but are different in other important respects. Mill suggests just that.

More precisely, one can extrapolate the following argument from Mill's discussions of "higher pleasures" and "individuality."[65] Human good or welfare (Mill uses the term "happiness") is not a simple matter of achieving satisfaction. Some pleasures or satisfactions or, more generally, achievements and activities are more valuable than others, not because of the intensity and duration of the pleasures they afford, but because they are the things that people with experience prefer. Informed judgment on such matters implies that happiness, or the best life for a human being, involves the development and exercise of peculiarly human capacities, such as planning, judgment, discrimination, and experimentation. Personal freedom is, then, important in two ways. First, one cannot develop such capacities without considerable freedom from the heavy hand of custom. Second, one cannot engage in those activities that are valuable in themselves, which are an essential part of happiness, without freedom from intervention. One must be free to experiment and strike out on one's own, partly in order to *find* the best way of life for oneself, but also because acting in that way *is* part of the best life for human beings.

This means that extensive personal freedom is not just a precondition for happiness – it is a permanent necessity. But if, at the same time, we can be justified in taking legal action to prevent people from harming others, then those actions must be severely limited, specifically to the prevention of harms that correspond to interests that all people have in common. If, however, we have sufficient knowledge of such interests to justify intervention, then we have sufficient knowledge to justify some paternalistic actions. In other words, this line of reasoning might limit paternalistic interference to the protection of those interests that all people have in common. Mill thus suggests the need to identify a limited class of publicly ascertainable "primary interests," the service of which is the only acceptable basis for social intervention. Some limited paternalistic intervention could then be justified, provided it was aimed at protecting the special class of universal primary interests. Beyond that, people should be left to work things out for themselves.

There is a further complication that might reinforce our qualms about paternalistic interference. That is the significance of individual choice or consent. There is a legal maxim to the effect that no wrong is done to one who consents: *volenti non fit injuria*. This suggests that some consideration should be given to a person's assumption of apparent risk. People have a wide range of interests, some of which conflict with others. Thus, a mountain climber usually appreciates the risk he takes, and is willing to accept it. Indeed, taking risks is sometimes an essential element of valued activities. In any case, an individual is often in the best position to judge whether the risk is outweighed by other interests that he has at stake. We may sometimes have enough understanding of those we know quite well to question such judgments, but most often – as Mill would insist – we are not in a good position to form such judgments about others. This complication is especially important because the clearest risks involve primary interests, such as life, health, and bodily integrity. When people who are not generally incompetent assume such risks, we must suppose that they do so for a reason they regard as adequate. Since these reasons are likely to involve further, idiosyncratic interests that they have, we are usually in a poor position to judge whether their assumption of such risks can be justified as serving their own best interests in the long run. We are too prone, Mill saw, to judge by our own lights, which are likely to be very different from theirs. That is, we are too prone to judge what is good for others on the basis of what we take to be good for ourselves. Because our judgment in such matters is unreliable, we have additional reason to hesitate from interfering, even when primary interests are at stake.

We began with the question whether Mill's principle of liberty could be defended, especially on utilitarian grounds. We have found that Mill's own argument is unsound, but that a more limited restriction on legal paternalism might be defended, given certain assumptions about what is good for human beings. These assumptions lead far from traditional utilitarianism, and they are no less controversial for that. And yet it is unclear how else to justify the view that limits should be placed on paternalistic intervention.

One might, of course, reject Mill's initial approach and try to argue from a basic general right to liberty. If each person has a right to make choices for herself, this must mean that interference cannot be justified merely in "cost-benefit" terms. If I have a right to speak my mind publicly on political matters, for example, then this means that interference with my so acting cannot be justified merely on the grounds that the benefits of interference can be expected to exceed the costs. To reason in that way is not to take the right at all seriously. Can the same be said of a general right to liberty?

If there is a general right to liberty in this sense, then utilitarian arguments for legal intervention can never be justified. That is, legal action can never be justified on the mere ground that its benefits are likely to exceed its costs. The stakes must be much higher: the prospective benefits must greatly exceed the costs. But this does not seem to square with our usual view of justified legal action. As Ronald Dworkin has observed, many routine legal regulations are justified in cost-benefit terms without any complaint about that mode of reasoning. The decision to restrict automotive traffic, so that it can go only one way on a street on which it formerly was allowed to travel in both directions, can be justified in cost-benefit terms, which suggests that no significant right is at stake – no right comparable to the right to speak one's mind publicly on political matters.[66] If any regulations which limit liberty can be justified merely on the ground that their benefits exceed their costs, then the general presumption favoring liberty is rather weak. If we wish to speak of a general right to liberty, then, we must acknowledge that it simply means that any limitation on our liberty requires some sort of justification. But, if restrictions can be justified on the mere ground that benefits are likely to exceed costs, then this right would be incapable of blocking utilitarian arguments for limiting liberty. It would provide no special objection to paternalistic intervention or to other limitations on liberty.

It is tempting to suggest an alternative approach. Our discussion of legal coercion led to the idea that the legal recognition of excusing conditions rests on the requirement of a "fair bargain" between the individual and the rest of the community. It is fair to impose a penalty for engaging in prohibited activities only if the individual was in fact capable of making a relevant choice. In that case, the individual could quite properly be held accountable for her behavior. The suggestion one might make here is that restrictions on legal paternalism constitute a complementary element of that bargain. Just as the individual can fairly be subjected to the legal consequences of her freely chosen behavior, so the individual must be understood to accept the personal risks – the nonlegal consequences – too. Only such an attitude on the part of the official organs of the community expresses the respect that individuals are due. By treating individuals differently, we imply that they are merely objects to be worked on for the purposes of social engineering. If we respect their capacity for self-governance, however, we are committed to respecting the choices that they make. This means punishing only when they are in control of their behavior. It also means assuming that they are capable of deciding what is best for themselves. Such reasoning would seem to warrant a strong presumption against paternalistic intervention.

The enforcement of morality

Even if we think there is a general right to liberty or a strong presumption against restricting it, we may not assume it covers the liberty to do wrong. Indeed, when law is judged in moral terms, it would seem to follow that the best grounds for legal intervention are moralistic – whatever else law may do, it should prevent immoral conduct. But Mill's doctrine of liberty seems to deny this. He says that one "cannot rightfully be compelled to do or forebear ... because, in the opinions of others, to do so would be wise or even right." Why should Mill, or anyone, take this position?

The general issue is of practical importance because of proposals that have been made, and sometimes adopted, to revise the criminal law either to permit acts that have been prohibited, apparently on moral grounds (a revision that would accord with Mill's position) or to prohibit acts, on moral grounds, that are now permitted (which conflicts with Mill's position). An example is homosexual acts performed by consenting adults in private. Mill's principle implies that such conduct may not be restricted on the ground that it is wrong.

Some of the recent public debate over this issue was sparked by Lord Devlin's claim that a government must regard itself as responsible for enforcing moral standards.[67] Devlin's position has been criticized by many who ally themselves with Mill, but there is confusion on both sides concerning what is at stake. Let us look first at Mill's position and then turn to the issues raised by Devlin.

Mill's own position invites confusion. While he objects to interfering with conduct on the ground that it is wrong, he nevertheless seems committed to the position that wrong conduct may be restricted. That is because the principle of liberty condones interference with conduct that causes harm to others, and Mill seems to hold that wrong conduct falls under that description. For Mill is a utilitarian, and he is committed to judging conduct by its effects on the general welfare. He is committed, roughly speaking, to judging conduct wrong when it fails to promote, or at least undermines, the general welfare. The clearest cases of such conduct would be acts that cause harm to others (without preventing greater harm), or in other words violations of our duties toward others, which require us to respect their interests. If restrictions on such conduct are effective, they discourage acts that cause harm to others, and might be justified on utilitarian grounds. But this is to justify restrictions on conduct that Mill, as a utilitarian, considers wrong.

Mill would not, of course, approve of restrictions on all such conduct. A utilitarian wishes legal intervention to serve the general welfare, but we cannot assume – and Mill does not assume – that legal interference with harmful or dangerous conduct will always serve the general welfare. This is because legal interference has costs as well as limited effectiveness; so it might do more harm than good. Furthermore, under Mill's principle of liberty, conduct may be restricted only for the purpose of preventing harm to others. Mill would not approve of legal interference with conduct that simply failed to promote happiness to the maximum degree possible. But, even if we limit legal intervention to the cases that could be justified under the principle of liberty, we would still restrict conduct that Mill considers wrong.

Mill, in fact, goes further in suggesting that immoral conduct may be restricted. He claims that calling an act wrong, or the breach of a moral obligation, implies that there is some justification for punishing a person who performs it, "if not by law, by the opinion of his fellow creatures; if not by opinion, by the reproaches of his own conscience ... Duty is a thing which may be *exacted* from a person, as one exacts a debt."[68] This suggests a presumption favoring the enforcement of morality, rather than the opposite – a presumption that may, of course, be rebutted, if enforcement would be counterproductive.

Mill's opposition to paternalistic intervention qualifies that presumption. Social interference should aim at preventing harm to people other than those whose conduct is restricted. For the sake of simplicity, let us ignore the qualifications that we found were needed by Mill's views about paternalism, and assume that Mill is opposed to all paternalistic intervention. If we combine this with his notion that "duty is a thing which may be exacted from a person," we find Mill with the position that there is a presumption favoring the enforcement of those duties that we have toward other people, duties that require us to respect their interests. On the surface, at least, this seems to clash with the idea that morality should not be enforced.

How, then, can we understand Mill's opposition to the

enforcement of morality? A two-step argument can be reconstructed. First, Mill's principle of liberty does not specify which acts may or may not be restricted, but concerns instead the proper grounds for legal intervention. This is suggested by his formulation of the principle and his treatment of paternalistic intervention. A given act might be interfered with on distinct and independent grounds. Smoking might be restricted for the purpose of preventing harm to smokers or preventing harm to others. Mill's principle of liberty implies that the latter aim is legitimate, but not the former. Similar considerations apply to the enforcement of morality. Homosexual acts might be restricted because they are believed to be wrong or as a way of preventing harm to others. Mill's principle of liberty implies that the latter aim is legitimate, but not the former. Mill's principle makes a practical difference in some cases, but not in all. That is, in some cases, the very conduct that some would wish to interfere with on paternalistic or moralistic grounds could also be restricted on the ground that it would prevent harm to others.

Second, Mill must believe that, by restricting the grounds of legal intervention to harm prevention, we would best serve the general welfare. He must believe that, if we justify interference on moralistic grounds, we would undermine the general welfare. This is presumably because the moral judgments that are enforced might be mistaken. It is not just that we might miscalculate the likely consequences of conduct, or of interference with it, by failing to take costs as well as benefits into account. We might judge by the wrong standards. Legislators seeking to enforce morality might prohibit acts that are mistakenly judged to be immoral. If they are not limited by the principle of liberty to interfering only when restrictions will prevent harm to others, their actions can be completely misguided, and liberty would then be restricted for no good purpose. To sanction the enforcement of morality is to open up the floodgates to unwarranted intervention.

Given this clarification of Mill's position, let us now consider Devlin's argument for the enforcement of morality.

Devlin's reasoning is not entirely clear, but we can identify some strands within it that merit comment. I shall mention three possible interpretations of Devlin's argument, one of which is closely related to Mill's own position.

Devlin seems to argue that a society cannot survive unless its government enforces moral standards for conduct. There are two ways of understanding this. On one interpretation, Devlin simply conceives of a society as identified by the moral standards that are widely accepted in it, so that any significant change in prevailing moral attitudes signals the transition from one "society" to another. Government enforcement of certain standards is required, on this view, just to preserve the identity of the society. We shall spend no more time on this version of Devlin's argument, for nothing of value seems at stake – only the maintenance of a stage in local history.

On a second interpretation, Devlin claims that, if a government fails to enforce moral standards, the result is a breakdown of social restraints and of practices that depend on mutual trust. There is an erosion of social order and cohesion. The community is then thrust into what some call a "state of nature," with the consequence of widespread suffering, which could have been avoided by effective governmental enforcement of moral standards. In other words, moral standards provide a kind of social cement which must be reinforced by official sanction. Enforcement is required to prevent harm. This is the version of the argument that relates closely to Mill's position.

A third interpretation of Devlin's argument is possible. On this view, what is at stake is not human welfare but what we might call moral legitimacy. A government is committed to certain values, which it employs to justify its uses of coercion. It loses legitimacy – the right to rule – unless it remains faithful to those standards by enforcing them rigorously. We shall turn to this type of argument later.

Let us consider how harm might be prevented by interference with conduct that some consider immoral. If homosexual acts performed in private by consenting adults cause harm that is limited to those who engage in them, then Mill's objection to paternalistic intervention comes into play: one may not interfere in order to prevent people from harming themselves. If the acts cause harm to others not engaged in the activities, then interference might be justified under the principle of liberty. But suppose that this is not the case. There remains a further possibility. Devlin claims that harm will *result* if governments do not enforce prevailing standards – harm that can be prevented by their enforcement. This may be possible, even if no harm is *caused* by acts that violate prevailing standards. And Mill would then seem committed, by his principle, to enforcing those standards, as Devlin urges. Let us consider why.

Although Mill sometimes seems to say that conduct may be restricted only if it *causes* or threatens harm to others, this cannot be his considered judgment on the matter, for it does not account for his own examples. He assumes that we are justified in requiring people to give testimony in court, and he treats this as if it did not violate his principle of liberty.[69] But we cannot assume that the failure to give testimony on request is harmful or dangerous to others. Although Mill's reasoning is unclear (and he may be confused about what is at stake in such examples), we can reconstruct an argument to account for this sort of example. The subpoena power is required for an effective system of criminal justice. If criminal law can be justified on the ground that it prevents harm to people other than those whose conduct is restricted, then so can the subpoena power; for all practical purposes, any justification of the former must include the latter. This is compatible with the principle of liberty, provided that we understand it to say that legal intervention can be justified, not only against acts that cause or threaten harm to others, but more generally on the ground that *it prevents harm* to people other than those whose conduct is restricted.

This reading of the principle of liberty renders it capable of justifying legal action in many cases. It is required, not just to account for the example of requiring people to give testimony in court, but for many other restrictions which prevent harm to others, such as traffic laws. These could be justified on the ground that they prevent harm to persons other than those whose conduct is restricted, though some of the acts that are prohibited, such as driving on the "wrong side" of the road, cannot be assumed to be more dangerous than the acts that are allowed by them. That is, driving on the "wrong side" of the road is dangerous only given the established practice of driving on the "right side" – a practice that is established by the traffic laws themselves. There is no right or wrong side of the road, in the relevant sense, until there are such laws.

This makes a great deal of difference to Mill's overall position. Mill would not limit legal action to the suppression of conduct that is harmful or dangerous to others. He would be prepared to entertain concerted legal efforts to prevent harm to people other than those whose conduct is restricted. If some people suffer as a consequence of poor housing, inadequate medical services, and other conditions that might be rectified most effectively by governmental programs, then Mill would presumably favor them, provided that the benefits exceed the costs. It does not matter who is responsible for bad conditions, or that anyone be responsible; what matters is that harm can be prevented.

Once we understand the principle of liberty in this way, we can see that the question it asks is not whether conduct is harmful or dangerous to others, but whether restriction of that conduct would prevent harm to people other than those whose conduct is restricted. We then find it capable, at least in principle, of accommodating Devlin's argument. For Devlin does not claim that conduct which is condemned as immoral by the standards that he wishes enforced is *itself* harmful or dangerous to others, but he does claim that enforcement of those standards is required to prevent harm to people in the society generally, and thus to prevent harm to others.

On this reading of Mill and Devlin, the dispute between them turns on complex and subtle but nevertheless empirically ascertainable matters of fact. This leaves us with the question whether Devlin's argument is sound. Is it true that the widely shared values within a society at a given time must be enforced in order to prevent a catastrophic breakdown of the social order?

It is unclear that we can give a sound general answer to this question, without considering different sets of circumstances. For example, one might reasonably suppose that it makes a difference what standards are to be enforced – what they require or allow and the more or less direct effects of enforcement. If the standards condemn conduct that is harmful or dangerous to others, and legal enforcement is required to insure compliance, then it is plausible to suppose that their enforcement is required to maintain social cohesion. But, if those standards have little to do with human welfare, except in a negative way by limiting our freedom to do as we wish, then that claim is much less plausible.

For Devlin's claim to appear plausible, we must imagine that the failure of the government to enforce moral standards generally leads to a breakdown of the social order. If we try to imagine a chain reaction of perceived injury, resentment, and mistrust so great that it destroys social stability, we find it easiest when significant interests are at stake – interests that are adversely affected by violations of those standards. In that case, however, the interests could presumably be protected by legal action that would be allowed by more straightforward application of the principle of liberty. But, if no significant interests are at stake, then it is unlikely (though not perhaps impossible) that people will react so strongly to violations of prevailing standards that they will lose all confidence in their neighbors and move into a "state of nature."

Devlin's argument is implausible because he seems to hold that the standards to be enforced need not be justifiable on grounds of harm prevention or, indeed, *any* other grounds. They must simply express intense unreflective attitudes, such as disgust.[70] But we have no reason to suppose that such standards must be backed by legal enforcement, lest law and order perish. Devlin seems to exaggerate the dependence of social stability on respect for standards that may be arbitrary.

It does not follow that no better argument can be constructed for the enforcement of moral standards that would be covered by Mill's principle. It is sometimes suggested, for example, that coercion can be justified by considerations of fair play. Suppose our community is short of water and that action must be taken to prevent a depletion of the supply. Time is short and technology is limited, so the community must rely on water rationing, which is not closely policed. People are asked not to use water for various inessential purposes, in order to insure that enough will be available for essential uses. Those who comply with these requests have good self-interested reasons for doing so, but they may also be resentful of anyone who takes advantage of widespread compliance with the rationing rules and uses extra water for his own private inessential purposes. Such a person is a "free-loader," taking more than his share of some "public good" that is made available only by the voluntary compliance of others. One may argue that anyone found taking more than his share should be punished.

This is a difficult case. It looks as if the argument for taking legal action against free-loaders is moralistic, based on the unfairness of their conduct. For it need not be assumed that the few who take advantage of others' compliance place the rationing system in jeopardy, so it need not be assumed that such action can be justified on the ground that it prevents harm to others. But the case is not so clear as that suggests. Any such arrangement is inherently unstable, in the sense that many may be tempted to take advantage of others' compliance and free-load, so that the rationing scheme collapses through inadequate compliance. In that case, all are likely to suffer. Legal action against free-loaders can then be justified on the ground that it insures stability and thus prevents harm to people other than those whose conduct is restricted. And it is unclear that legal action could be justified when it is certain that free-loading would do no harm. This is not to say that

free-loading would then be condoned – for that would likely
render the arrangement unstable; and in any case there may be
good moral grounds for condemning the conduct of free-
loaders as unfair. It is one thing, however, to *condemn*
free-loading as unfair; it is quite another to *punish* free-loading
when it is certain to do no harm. Mill would presumably say
that our inclination to punish free-loading could be justified on
the ground that it must often be discouraged, in order to
prevent harm to others. And he is not clearly wrong.

Similar problems concern the enforcement of rights. It is
often assumed that claims of right provide an argument for
enforcement – that legal action can be justified on the ground
that it prevents violations of rights. One might wonder,
however, whether such arguments would seem plausible if
significant interests were not at stake. Indeed, we rarely claim
rights in other cases. Mill would presumably say that our
inclination to approve of the enforcement of rights could be
justified on the ground that valid claims of right concern
important interests, so that their protection prevents harm to
others.

These arguments do not show that coercive intervention can
be justified only for the purpose of preventing harm to others.
But they do suggest the plausibility of that position. Moral
arguments for taking legal action are most plausible when that
action would prevent harm to persons other than those whose
conduct is restricted; they are much less plausible in other
cases.

One qualification should be added. We have been using
"interests" loosely here, and it is not clear that all the interests
that we believe on reflection should be protected are those that
would be acknowledged by a utilitarian. It may be argued, for
example, that human dignity is an interest that should be
protected by legal action, though it does not fit neatly into
utilitarian calculations of welfare. (Mill might recognize the
importance of human dignity. But, as we have already noted,
his conception of human happiness is much broader than that
of traditional utilitarianism.) At the same time, however, it

should be noted that the grossest violations of human dignity, such as systematic discrimination on the basis of race, sex, class, religion, and national origin, are typically coupled with systematic frustration of those very interests that must enter into any plausible conception of human welfare.

As we noted earlier, Devlin suggests a third line of argument for the enforcement of morality, where not human welfare but the right to rule is at stake. A permissive attitude toward immoral conduct undermines the right to rule. Devlin claims, for example, that the government of the United Kingdom is committed to the principles of Christian morality. Unless it appealed to some such principles, it could not claim the right to rule; but, once it relies on some set of principles, it is committed to enforcing them in general.

This argument begs the question. For the principles of Christian morality may set limits on the proper role of government, by implying that a government must not infringe certain freedoms. While it may be argued that people have no right to engage in immoral conduct, it does not follow that anyone else, including public officials, has the right to interfere. Moreover, Devlin gives no reason to suppose that the values he believes a government should enforce have any standing, since they are simply the expression of unreflective attitudes held by typical citizens, which need not correspond to standards of, say, Christian morality. Furthermore, Devlin puts himself in a bad position to defend the right to rule. For he seems skeptical about the possibility of defending moral judgments. If values are regarded as arbitrary, then no credit can be given to a government's claim to have the right to rule.

It is sometimes suggested that a government has the responsibility to promote the moral virtue of its citizens. This may be the sort of position that Devlin wishes to embrace. But, if this is used to defend the enforcement of morality against claims that the proper role of government is limited, it too begs the question at issue. In order to appraise such a position, we need to know what standards of moral virtue are claimed to be sound, and to be shown that they do not limit the proper role of government in relation to personal choice. We shall examine a particular version of this theory in the next section.

Public morality and speech

Some of those who claim that a government has an obligation to promote the moral virtue of its citizens, and thus to enforce sound moral standards, raise a different sort of issue concerning political morality – one that concerns the nature of political argument. I have in mind those who claim some special, privileged access to the principles of political morality (or morality in general). Such a position appears to be endorsed by many religious "fundamentalists," who place great stock in revelation or the inspired interpretation of sacred texts. It is not, however, limited to contemporary fundamentalists, but is shared, for example, by those who accept Plato's vision of the ideal commonwealth, which was to be governed absolutely by a caste of "philosopher kings" who alone have access to the otherwise inaccessible principles of virtue.[71] On this sort of view, moral guidance is revealed to a select few, and political argument is not public.

To understand this position better, we may recall John Austin's conception of morality. Austin held that moral obligations are determined by God's will, which is inaccessible to ordinary observation. But Austin did not maintain that we should allow ourselves to be led by those who claim privileged access to God's will. Instead, he argued that, since God must be understood to wish us well, the criterion of obligation must be the service of human welfare. Thus, despite his theistic conception of morality, Austin held, in effect, that political decisions should turn on natural facts about human beings and the empirically observable consequences of actions.

In this respect, Austin's approach to political morality is much like Mill's. Mill can be understood to hold that principles of political morality should be grounded on a naturalistic conception of value. Human good and harm are determined by ordinary empirical facts about human beings, and justified decisions take only such facts into account. More generally, the arguments that may be used to appraise decisions turn entirely on considerations that are accessible to all persons. Political argument is, in this sense, public. We need no leap of faith or revelation, no special class or caste, to seek out moral truths that are obscure to ordinary people.

One need not be a utilitarian to have this conception of political morality. Rawls, for example, holds that political principles must be acceptable to free and equal persons who deliberate about the ground rules for their social institutions. This does not require that one reject religious beliefs or institutions generally, as Rawls makes clear, though it means that one cannot give credence to a select class of moral authorities on political matters. And, just as one who endorses a naturalistic and public conception of political principles can retain his own religious views (so long as they are compatible with this conception), he can also embrace moral standards based on faith or revelation, provided that he does not seek to impose them on other persons.

The contrast, then, is this. Whatever one may think about the ultimate foundation of value, indeed whatever one may think about the substance of one's moral obligations, one may hold that matters of political morality must be regulated by principles that employ naturalistic criteria; or one may deny this. One may hold that political questions are to be settled by arguments that are inherently public; or one may deny this. This contrast seems to underlie some disputes concerning the enforcement of morality. Some, like Mill, insist that legal interference with personal decisions must be defended in terms that make public debate and objective decisions possible. Others believe, by contrast, that their superior insight into moral matters or the insight of those whom they regard as specially privileged moral authorities must be allowed to decide such issues. One need not be a utilitarian, one need not accept the principle of liberty, to question the latter sort of claim.

We have assumed throughout this study that deliberation on moral and political matters is accessible to all normally competent persons. There are differences among us, but these generally concern the facility with which we grasp the import of an argument. Some people are unable to follow abstract reasoning at all, but this is a deficiency in mental capacity, not a matter of exclusion from a select group who are endowed with inexplicable moral insight. We have assumed that moral deliberation, like scientific practice, is open to all as a matter of principle. Justifications for political positions are accessible to all. One who rejects a naturalistic and public conception of political morality seems to reject such an approach to moral deliberation on matters of mutual concern, and to reject the idea that what is done to people by other people needs to be defended in terms that all can understand, on the basis of principles that all are capable of applying. To reject these ideas is to deny the essential spirit of democracy.

This discussion provides a necessary background for the last problem of liberty on our list, that of free expression. We shall consider this issue briefly.

Mill undertakes to show why it is "imperative that human beings should be free to form opinions and to express their opinions without reserve."[72] First, no one is infallible; so no one has the right to decide what others may be allowed to hear or believe; for he may be wrong. Second, even if an opinion is wrong, it may contain some element of truth which can only emerge in open discussion of the conflicting opinions. Third, the rational grounds for holding an opinion can be discovered only through open discussion so, if we wish to have reasoned opinion rather than mere prejudice, we must allow opinions to be tested in that way. Fourth, we can neither fully understand the beliefs we hold nor be motivated to act on them without a full appreciation of their rational grounds.

Although this line of reasoning is roughly utilitarian, because Mill holds that open discussion is needed to reach well-grounded opinion and effective practice, no explicit connection is made to the promotion of welfare. Perhaps Mill assumes there is such a connection. His failure to rely on narrowly utilitarian considerations, however, can only make his view more broadly appealing, provided that we value both well-grounded opinions and informed, effective practice and can accept his factual assumptions.

Mill seems at first to ignore the harms that can be done by expressions of opinion. In a later passage, however, he admits that expressions of opinion can "without justifiable cause do harm to others" that might warrant legal interference.[73] The upshot is that Mill's defense of freedom of opinion and its expression is qualified by the principle of liberty, which says that legal intervention can be justified in order to prevent harm to others.

That freedom of opinion and its expression merits protection, though interference with it can sometimes be justified, is hardly controversial. The difficulty is determining where to draw the line. No matter how much value we place on open discussion, it cannot be denied that serious harm can sometimes result from public speech. Panic can be caused, riots incited, reputations ruined, and fair trials hindered by malicious, negligent, and even innocent expressions of opinion, both true and false.

The underlying difficulty is determining the grounds for protecting speech in relation to the special role of governments. Mill's approach suggests that officials are constantly faced with the need to balance considerations of utility in order to determine when public speech should be left unhindered or restricted. That approach would not support the belief that speech should be protected as a right, as it is, for example, in the US Constitution. For, once it is established as a right, officials should not regard themselves as free to decide such questions by balancing considerations of utility. If freedom of speech is a right, then it may be restricted only to prevent grave dangers or to protect overriding rights that are clearly threatened.

Mill could be understood to argue for a stronger protection of free speech. It is plausible to claim that governments cannot by and large be trusted to exercise discretion in this area soundly and with due concern for the general welfare.

Governmental policies are too systematically self-serving. While the costs of leaving speech unfettered are sometimes considerable, the costs of leaving it unprotected by an established right are even greater.

Our discussion of political morality may suggest further reasons for wishing to protect free speech. Political argument is fundamentally public. Legal decisions and govermental policy must be subjected to appraisal in open discussion on the basis of criteria that can be understood by all. Those in power have no special claim to moral insight from which others generally are barred. They have privileged access to information that is needed for responsible judgment, but there is rarely good reason to keep such information secret. On the contrary, they have the obligation (whether or not it is established in law) to disseminate such information, promote discussion, and encourage reasoned deliberation. Protection of expression as a right is a necessary (though by no means sufficient) means to insure that governments live up to this obligation.

7

The rule of law

Much of what seems distinctive and is thought valuable about law as we know it concerns procedures. The process of adjudication, for example, is valued as a means of settling disputes in a regular, peaceful manner, according to rules that have already been laid down. Even when established rules are unclear, adjudication, at its best, is thought to serve important values such as rationality, impartiality, fairness, and consistency. So far as legal procedures serve such values, they are often thought of as deserving respect, independently of the outcome of the legal process.

In this chapter we shall complete our survey of issues in normative jurisprudence by examining the values that may be exemplified in legal processes – values that are often thought of as defining "the rule of law." Then we shall turn, finally, to the idea of obedience to law – another requirement that is associated with the rule of law.

Process values and institutional structures

In an earlier discussion, we took note of the distinction between the justice of laws and the justice of their application. We observed that these appear somewhat independent, since both just and unjust laws can be applied either fairly or unfairly. Our concern was to consider possible connections between the concept of law and justice in the application of the law to particular cases. Our concern now is different: to understand how desirable legal *procedures* are related to the desirable *results* or consequences of those procedures. Justice is one value with which we are concerned, but not the only one, for both procedures and their outcomes can be appraised in other terms, and we wish the present discussion to be as neutral as possible with respect to competing theories about the values that ought to be served by law.

Our problem is suggested by Rawls's distinctions between "perfect," "imperfect," and "pure" procedural justice. The concepts of perfect and imperfect justice apply to procedures when the justice of their outcomes is independent of the procedures themselves. Perfect procedural justice is possible when we can devise a procedure that is guaranteed to achieve just outcomes; otherwise only imperfect procedural justice is possible. The concept of pure procedural justice applies when the justice of an outcome is determined by the fairness of the procedure, as in the case of a fair lottery.

These distinctions may suggest that legal procedures, be they legislative or adjudicative, must always be judged by reference to results or consequences. We evaluate legislation, for example, in terms of the benefits and burdens they bring and the way these are distributed. In a similar way, we appraise litigation in terms of the soundness of decisions, its contribution to social harmony, and the like. This makes it natural to suppose that legal procedures ought to be judged in terms of the values that we ought to seek in their results, and that they can have no other value. In other words, it is natural to suppose that legal procedures fall under the concept of imperfect procedural justice – because we can judge the outcomes independently of the processes, which cannot generally guarantee desirable outcomes.

This conception of the value that legal procedures might embody is reinforced by some widely accepted normative theories, such as utilitarianism. Legal procedures are preliminary to authoritative legal decisions and, according to theories like utilitarianism, decisions should be judged by their effects. It seems to follow that, on such a view, legal procedures should be judged by their tendency to yield desirable results.

But this approach tends to obscure both the complexity and the importance of legal procedures. Even if we assume that procedures, like law in general, should be judged in instrumental terms, we must acknowledge that they might have distinctive effects. For example, well-designed procedures might encourage respect for law, and thus obedience to law, which many believe is a good thing. Many believe that law provides peaceful ways of settling disputes, makes social life less dangerous than it would otherwise be, and facilitates mutually beneficial cooperation. We can agree, even if we caution that law does not automatically serve such ends and does not always do so as well as it should.

Let us assume that law should generally be judged by its service of some overarching values, such as welfare, equality, or specific rights, and that legal procedures can likewise be judged, directly or indirectly, in such terms. Two further possibilities should be considered. One is that there may be values that procedures ought to respect, which serve as limiting principles without determining more generally the direction that law ought to take. Another is that there may be values, such as fairness, which legal procedures ought to embody independently of desirable outcomes.

Our strategy for exploring these possibilities is the following. We shall assume that law ought to serve some overarching values and consider their implications for the design of legal procedures. We begin, in other words, by adopting the standpoint of law makers, without limiting ourselves to substantive legislation. Then we shall take the standpoint of people subjected to legal procedures, whose cases are "processed" in them. This will enable us to consider the moral faults that may be found in legal procedures and their implications for procedural design. The combination of these two approaches will help us determine how much of what we ought to seek in the qualities of legal procedures can be accounted for in instrumental terms, and how much has independent foundations.

Suppose that we are legislators fully empowered to shape the law as we wish, but committed to serving the values that law ought to serve, whatever they might be. How should we proceed? Whatever values we might wish to serve, we will most likely lay down general standards that are couched in familiar terms. They will not simply say "avoid harm," "respect others' rights," and the like, but will indicate types of acts that are generally to be performed or avoided. For one thing, our legislation will be limited. Because restrictions and enforcement have significant costs, we will not wish to make all undesirable behavior either punishable or subject to civil remedies. And we will be working with limited information, so we will limit our legislation to some standards the results of which we can reliably predict. Also, some of our legislation is likely to create new practices, as traffic laws do, and this cannot be done by using such formulas as "avoid harm" or "respect rights." Finally, by referring to familiar types of behavior, we will provide standards that ordinary people can use to guide their own conduct.

We will also be concerned with the application of these standards, since we shall assume that they are applied, as legal standards usually are, not just by those whose behavior is to be guided by them, but also by those who must make authoritative determinations about whether they were followed or violated. Assuming that we are legally empowered to decide this, we are likely to design procedures for the application of such standards on the assumption that other officials will be charged with the task of their administration. For we will not have the time to function as both legislators and administrators; in any case, if we legislate well, our laws should outlast us. We will also wish to have specialists who are suited for the job made responsible for adjudication. For that task is not mechanical. The standards that we lay down will not always be adequately clear, and it will be desirable to have authoritative interpretations made of them as required. And, since how the law applies depends essentially on the facts, we will wish to construct procedures that promote the maximum feasible collection and marshaling of relevant information, so that authoritative judgments can be made on the most informed basis possible. Since evidence is often compatible with contradictory factual conclusions, and judgment is required to make a reasonable assessment of the evidence, the procedures that we design should encourage their rational appraisal, leading to conclusions that can be justified. Furthermore, human character is fallible and judgment can be affected in subtle ways by prejudice and special interest, so procedures should be contrived to compensate for these factors, in part by testing the neutrality and impartiality of adjudicators. Partly to compensate for these human limitations, we might also require that courts defend their interpretations of the law by reasoned argument, taking into account considerations that can be marshaled on both sides. This will also provide a better basis for subsequent understanding of the law, as well as for criticism of it with an eye to further legislation. And, to help insure that the entire process proceeds according to the standards that we lay down, we may wish to require that competent counsel represent each side of the dispute or prosecution, or at least that competent counsel be available.

We might summarize these reflections on desirable characteristics of legal procedures under the heading of "procedural rationality." The procedures should be maximally reliable methods for arriving at the decisions that we are mandating in our substantive standards. They should aim at accuracy and should promote authoritative determinations that are justifiably regarded as accurate. This is a matter of procedural rationality because it is aimed at insuring that the values *to be* served by the substantive standards *will actually* be served. Legislators can reasonably select and design such standards only when they can make reliable predictions about the effects of their legislation, and they cannot generally make such predictions unless they can rely upon those who are charged with applying the standards to follow them. Furthermore, the rules may be contrived to serve those values indirectly, in a way that will not be apparent to one who simply understands what the rules generally require and allow. This is especially the case when the rules establish new practices, but it can apply to other rules as well. If the substantive rules to be applied are justifiable by reference to the values that they ought to serve, we must assume that an official who deviates from them does so only at the risk of undermining the rules and thus the values that they are designed to serve.

This means, however, that the internal organization of the law is most reasonably designed, from a legislative point of view, only if its procedures leading to authoritative applications make little direct reference to the values that the substantive rules ought overall to serve. The substantive rules of the criminal law, for example, might be designed to serve human welfare by promoting personal security and protecting certain specially important interests, to secure a set of recognized rights, or to enforce some acknowledged moral principles. But the procedures of the criminal law should insure, as far as possible, that those who are charged, tried, convicted, and punished for crimes include those, and only those, who have actually committed them. An official who is charged with applying the criminal law should generally be preoccupied with fidelity to its rules and should not attempt to deal with cases by seeking to serve the values that the rules are designed to serve. This is, of course, only a first approximation, from which the complexities of practice may require deviation. Because the standards may be unclear, it may be necessary to consider their aims in order to apply them intelligently. Furthermore, those charged with applying the law must often decide how to allocate their scarce resources, and this too will require them to consider the aims of the rules to be applied, the relative importance of the interests to be served, and so on. But officials who apply the rules must generally take care not to confuse their roles with that of the legislator, lest they undermine the very values to be served by the law they are applying. Procedures should constrain officials accordingly.

This helps us understand some aspects of "the rule of law" and the place of legal procedures within it. Whatever else this idea may suggest, it seems to include two essential elements: that decisions should be made according to existing law, and that they should be made on the merits of the alternatives. These two elements are not independent for, so far as the first is possible to satisfy, it presumably determines what counts as "the merits." According to this ideal, therefore, legal procedures should be designed so as to insure that decisions follow the law. The ideal takes on substance once we begin to reflect on the complexity of institutional design and law application. For law works through the medium of decisions made by human beings. Public officials alone are authorized to make certain decisions, and legal procedures, which precede their decisions, can be designed to constrain them in certain ways. From the standpoint of a legislator who shapes his law to serve important ends, an applicational decision should be guided by the law to be applied. Desirable procedures should insure scrupulous adherence to the law by requiring the collection of relevant information, and by compensating for human fallibility, as far as that is feasible. This does not mean that officials should apply the law unthinkingly, for an understanding of the law will aid in its intelligent application. But officials who apply problematic law should be required to make publicly clear what they are doing and how they arrive at their controversial decisions.

From the standpoint of an idealized legislator, therefore, "the rule of law" is a desirable ideal. Though it is distinct from the values to be served through legislation, it can be justified by reference to the service of those values.

But the picture so far is too simple. In the first place, institutional design does not begin and end with ordinary legislation. Just as the decisions of those who apply law can be constrained by legislatively imposed procedures, the decisions of legislators can be limited by constitutional arrangements. In the second place, while fidelity to law on the part of officials may serve the aims of legislation, it does not follow that it is required solely by such considerations. There seem to be quite independent moral objections to official deviation from law that is to be applied.

Certain values might best be served, not directly through the medium of legislation, but rather by more basic institutional design. It may be thought desirable, for example, to entrench some rights within the legal system by according them constitutional status, so that they serve as limits on permissible legislation. As Mill's theory of liberty suggests, even those whose normative theories are completely outcome-oriented may come to this conclusion. Thus, one might argue that welfare is most securely served by insuring that certain interests be immune to legislative intervention. Some constitutional provisions, however, are more plausibly (and at least in part) explained by reference to distinct values, such as the autonomy of the individual, which do not themselves determine a general direction for legislation but function instead as moral limits on it. This applies, for example, to prohibitions on *ex post facto* law and the "presumption of innocence" doctrine. Some of these values are reflected in legal procedures. Thus, constitutional limitations on "unreasonable searches and seizures" seem to reflect a concern, not just to limit police power, but to protect the privacy of the individual; and this is reflected, in turn, by the "exclusionary rule," which holds that evidence which would otherwise be admissible in a criminal trial may not be used if it was collected through illegal police activity.

Some reasons for wishing officials to be faithful to the law are grounded on moral considerations. Considerations of fairness and autonomy, for example, argue against penalizing people for doing what they had no reason to believe would be punishable. More generally, an official may have accepted a public trust that he would be faithful to the law. The resulting obligation has special importance in relation to some of the values that the law might be supposed to serve. For, as we have seen, a utilitarian who has undertaken to apply the law will have an uncertain commitment to abiding by its rules, even if he believes that they can be justified on utilitarian grounds. His utilitarian commitments will incline him to deviate from the law, whenever he has reason to believe that welfare would be better served by doing so. In general, if the values to be served by the rules are done so only contingently and instrumentally, someone who accepts those values may be tempted to deviate from the rules whenever he has reason to believe that they could be better served by deviation from them. If we believe, however, that officials have an obligation of fidelity to law which excludes such behavior, then we have further grounds for wishing to constrain official decisions by procedures that promote adherence to the law.

The obligation of fidelity to law has wider significance than this might suggest. When the law to be applied cannot be justified on its merits, then considerations of procedural rationality lose force and cannot support arguments to the effect that officials should follow the law and that procedures should insure that they do so. But it is generally understood that an official's obligation of fidelity to law is not so strongly dependent on the justifiability of the law to be applied. An official can be morally obligated, by virtue of his undertaking to apply the law as he finds it, to adhere to the law even when he judges (perhaps soundly and with justified confidence) that the law is defective.

It was argued earlier that this obligation has substantive limits – that it cannot be understood to cover every law, no matter how unjust or inhumane, in all circumstances. This is compatible, however, with the obligation covering laws that are unjustifiable on their merits. So, if we think that there are good grounds for procedures that promote official adherence to the law *even when* it is morally deficient, then we must rely on arguments like this, which go beyond considerations of procedural rationality and rest on independent moral consid-erations.

This brings us to the second aspect of our strategy for appraising legal procedures: adopting the standpoint of one whose case is processed. If we wish to understand what procedures should be like if they are to respect the rights of individuals, we can ask what such a person might reasonably complain about if he loses and believes soundly and with justified confidence that the outcome is wrong. (Such a person might be convicted of a crime or might, as either plaintiff or defendant, lose a suit for civil remedies.) If legal procedures are to be defensible from *his* point of view, he must not be able to blame his loss *on them*, but must attribute it to other factors. These might include his own inability to establish the merit of his case because of the lack of available evidence, which makes an unfavorable judgment reasonable under the circumstances, or some other unfortunate circumstance that could not have been prevented by better-designed procedures. He should not be able to complain that he could not understand the law (or could not get help in understanding it), that he was not informed of the complaint against him or the character of the reply, that he had no opportunity to present his case effectively, that the proceedings were biased against him. In short, there should be reasonable grounds for the belief that he had a full and fair hearing and that the final decision was (so far as one can tell) based on the merits of the opposing positions.

It is unclear that procedural *fairness*, as such, requires *more* than this. Other protections of the individual, such as the presumption of innocence in criminal prosecutions, may be morally important, but they do not seem to reflect the ordinary notion of procedural fairness. They become relevant to fairness only indirectly, when one is treated differently from others and denied such consideration.

What this suggests, however, is that procedural fairness converges with the requirements of procedural rationality, which in turn suggests that the former is reducible to or derived from the latter and has no independent value. This suspicion is encouraged by the difficulty we are likely to have in accounting for the requirements of procedural fairness on the basis of some other value that it regularly serves.

It may be suggested, for example, that procedural fairness respects the value of participation in the governance of one's community, which some believe is a good in itself. However, participation in the procedures that are used to apply the law seems markedly different from participation in the process that generates the law to be applied. Moreover *mere* participation in the former can be secured without providing a full and fair hearing for both sides, so an appeal to the value of participation generates no clear argument for our ordinary criteria of procedural fairness.

Perhaps part of the reason why procedural fairness is important but difficult to explain is that it has a looser but still important connection with other values. Its denial often constitutes an identifiable insult to the individual – an expression of the notion that one need not be heard or given equal consideration because one is assumed to be unreliable or less worthy of concern and respect. Such attitudes seem to have been embodied, for example, in the rules that permitted American courts to discount or exclude testimony from blacks.

That procedural fairness is a value somewhat *separate* from procedural rationality may be supported by further argument. First, our discussion of procedural rationality assumed that legislative aims, because they are served in a complex manner and sometimes only indirectly through general rules, are best served at the applicational level only by adherence to those rules. This is a contingent claim, about the way in which values are best served within complex institutional arrangements, and it may not hold true in all cases. Thus, for some values that legislators may wish to serve, and in some circumstances, procedural rationality might permit greater discretionary judgment at the applicational level or decisions that are made without a full and fair hearing of both sides. But our ordinary notion of procedural fairness seems to imply that *any* denial of a full and fair hearing would be objectionable, *even if* it served some legitimate legislative end.

Second, when legislative aims are best served by procedures that involve the full presentation of evidence and argument from both sides, then rules *requiring* both sides to participate fully might be defended in such terms. But procedural *fairness* does not *require* the individual to participate, though it requires that the individual have the *opportunity* to participate if she chooses. In other words, procedural fairness seems to imply that the individual has a right, which she might wish to waive. One must have the opportunity, but need not avail oneself of it. Suppose I am a defendant in a criminal trial, and have evidence that would establish my innocence, but decline to introduce it because it would hurt someone whose welfare is more important to me than the consequences of conviction. Considerations of procedural rationality would argue just as strongly for the introduction of such evidence, but procedural fairness is not offended in the least by my decision not to use it. Since procedural *rationality* and procedural *fairness* can diverge in this way, they seem morally distinguishable.

Let us turn now to the procedures that lead to legislative decisions. If we believe that law should serve important values, such as welfare, equality, or specific moral rights, then it would be natural to suppose that legislative decisions should aim directly at promoting those values, that legislators should be firmly committed to implementing them, and therefore that the rules determining who shall serve as legislators should select those with the appropriate commitments. But this approach ignores several complicating factors.

First, as we have noted, though some values are best served by legislation, others are better secured through constitutional arrangements that place limits on legislation. This is true of, but not limited to, important personal rights. The effect of such arrangements is to limit the direct pursuit by legislatures of the very values that are to be served by the system as a whole.

Second, the law, while important, is just one among several basic institutions and might best play a limited direct role, complementary to, say, the economic system. Even a utilitarian might hold that law should aim at serving more specific ends than human welfare in general, such as personal security, a minimum floor of welfare for all, the enforcement of private arrangements, and the maintenance of free and fair competition.

Third, as we have also noted, it may be held that legal intervention should be limited by certain principles, such as personal autonomy, which set no general direction for legislation. If we wish to respect such principles, we shall not wish to have a system that is maximally efficient in the promotion of overarching values. We shall be prepared to sacrifice efficiency for the sake of respecting personal rights. Legislation and procedures should be modified accordingly.

Such principles contribute to our ideals of due process and legality. The minimum standards of behavior should be followable, and limits should be placed on the state's use of its investigative powers, in order to maintain respect for the integrity and privacy of the individual.

Fourth, it is not always clear how to design a set of institutions so as to make them most effective means for promoting general values. To some extent, this reflects the complexity of institutions and the inevitable interaction of legal forms and social conditions. Needs, resources, traditions, and attitudes vary from one community to another, and what works best in one place may be ill suited to differing conditions. Even within a given social setting, there is room for considerable disagreement concerning how best to serve a given set of values.

Finally, we may wish to minimize an initial commitment to an overarching set of values and rely instead, to a significant degree, on political processes for determining the direction that legislation should take. For one thing, we have no clearly developed and adequately defended conception of the values that should set the direction of our institutions. Political philosophy, which represents our continuing attempt to work out such principles, has so far been more effective in justifying a commitment to specific principles, such as those that should limit coercion, than in establishing an overarching set of values. Furthermore, in actual practice we find ourselves within communities that are morally and politically hetero-geneous, where we can expect agreement on some important matters and disagreement on others. We therefore need a system that reflects some common aims but also respects the differences that persist among members of the community.

These considerations suggest the desirability of a system that sets limits on legal intervention and promotes effective, widespread political participation. They are reinforced by independent arguments from diverse political sources. Many utilitarians believe, for example, that the most effective, practical, or only intelligible way of insuring that institutions serve the general welfare is by making them reflect, as far as possible, the preferences of those who are governed. In short, a participatory democracy – and, by extension, as a "second-best" alternative for large and complex societies, representative democracy – is conceived of as the best means of insuring that authoritative decisions will serve the general welfare, or as the only way of making practical sense of that objective. At the same time, utilitarians like Mill have made a plausible case for setting limits on majority rule by means of constitutional protections for the individual and limitations on legislative discretion. Many nonutilitarians also believe that effective, widespread political participation combined with limits on legal action is required to serve such values as individual autonomy and cooperation.

This is somewhat vague, and two further comments may prevent misunderstanding. First, these remarks are meant to suggest that well-designed procedures are important in the political as well as the narrowly legal realm – procedures that insure, as far as possible, effective participation by an informed community. The least that we can do, and sometimes the best that we can do, is insure by our procedures that decisions will be deliberately made and argued for persuasively, in a public forum, by those authorized to make them.

Second, these remarks are not offered as an apology for any social system with which we are likely to be familiar. One trouble with using terms like "democracy" is that they might suggest the contrary, for they have been devalued by their application to systems that incorporated chattel slavery and disenfranchised even larger portions of the population, and to systems that fail to promote effective, widespread political pàrticipation.

To emphasize this point, we should note the relevance of economic arrangements. First, political power generally follows economic power, so a community must be economically much more egalitarian than those with which we are familiar if it is to promote widespread and effective participation in governance. Second, a large portion of many people's lives is occupied with economic activity within units from whose governance they are excluded. This not only affects adversely their conditions of work and of life in general, it also conflicts with some of the values we may well wish our social arrangements to serve, such as individual autonomy, cooperation, and welfare itself. Such values cannot be well served in either the political or economic realm unless familiar economic arrangements are modified drastically.

Obedience to law

Bentham expressed a standard attitude toward obedience to law when he wrote, "Under a government of laws, what is the motto of a good citizen? *To obey punctually; to censure freely.*"[74] It is widely believed that citizens (and, more generally, residents and visitors) of a community are morally bound to obey the law. This opinion is sometimes made part of the very notion of "the rule of law." It is the final topic to which we now turn.

The idea that there is a general obligation to obey the law does not refer to *merely* "legal obligations," when the latter correspond to every requirement and prohibition that are laid down by the law of a community. For laws are morally fallible, and cannot always be justified on their merits. The idea of a general obligation to obey the law is a claim about our moral responsibilities. It means that there is a moral obligation to obey the law even when the law is morally deficient.

We have touched upon this topic several times, so my position will come as no surprise. It is that we have no automatic obligation to obey the law. But the two opposing views need more deliberate explanation and evaluation.

The idea of a general obligation to obey the law requires clarification. We shall try to frame the most plausible, most easily defensible, least demanding version of that doctrine, in order to appraise it fairly. First, consider what it means to speak of a moral obligation. I take it that, when we speak of someone's having (or being under) a moral obligation, we mean, most generally, that there is a significant moral reason for behaving in a certain way – a reason that might have any number of foundations. In the absence of countervailing considerations, one who fails to discharge, meet, or live up to an obligation does wrong. It is necessary to consider the possibility of "countervailing considerations," because moral obligations can conflict, in which case one should presumably act so as to respect the more important obligation (or set of obligations). Thus, obligations can be "stronger" or "weaker" in the sense that some obligations can override others. An obligation which can never be overridden we can call "absolute." Ordinary obligations are rarely thought of as absolute, in this sense. To suppose, then, that one *cannot* be morally justified in disobeying the law is to suppose that the obligation to obey the law is absolute, and can never be overridden.

Second, the idea of a "general" obligation to obey the law means, in part, that one is morally bound to obey *all* the laws that apply to one and, furthermore, that *everyone* has such an obligation – that there is no one to whom this obligation does not apply (at least no one who comes under the governance of a legal system). But it may also be understood to mean something more: that the obligation obtains in *all* circumstances, without exception. This is what I mean by speaking of an "automatic" obligation to obey the law.

To suppose that one cannot be morally justified in disobeying the law is to suppose that the obligation to obey the law is not only absolute but also most general. A moment's reflection reveals that this is an extraordinary claim. Since obligations can conflict, and one might well be under an obligation to do something that involves disobedience to law, the claim implies that the obligation to obey the law outweighs all other moral considerations. But it seems just as reasonable to suppose that other obligations can outweigh any obligation one might have to obey the law. Indeed, since law is morally fallible, it seems more plausible to assume initially that there is *no* automatic obligation to obey the law, and certainly none that could be absolute. Since law is morally fallible, there must be special reasons to support the moral requirement that one obey the law.

Consider a law that requires one to inform police of any criticism of the current regime, and suppose that heavy penalties are prescribed for such criticisms. Suppose that a friend has, in confidence (before one is able to stop him), expressed an unfavorable judgment of the regime, precisely because it has enacted such a law. It is plausible to suppose that considerations of friendship and confidentiality argue against informing the police of that conversation, and thus that any obligation one might have to obey the law can conflict with other moral obligations, and may be outweighed by them. The idea that one can never be morally justified in disobeying the law denies this possibility. It thus seems much too "strong."

A more plausible, more easily defensible version of the claim that there is a *general* obligation to obey the law would construe the obligation as *non*absolute. It would hold that there is always a moral obligation to obey the law, a significant moral reason to obey, but it would allow that in some circumstances one might be morally justified in disobeying the law. This is the version of the claim that we must consider. If this version of the claim cannot be defended, then the stronger version must also be wrong.

The same example suggests, however, that even this weaker, more plausible version of the claim is dubious. Why should we suppose that there is *always* a moral obligation to obey the law – one that covers such oppressive and objectionable laws, and even worse laws, which we need not strain credibility to imagine, but can give instances of from past and present history? The burden of proof would seem to fall on anyone who wishes to assert there is even a "weak" moral obligation to obey the law.

To put this differently, because law is morally fallible, the claim that there is a general moral obligation to obey the law requires positive support. It stands in need of justification. This is not to say that justification is impossible, only that it cannot be taken for granted.

Political and legal theory have not neglected this problem, for they have suggested several different reasons for believing that there is a general obligation to obey the law. We shall examine some of these arguments, without pretending to make a comprehensive survey, for the objection to them is easily understood and can be summarized in advance: the reasons that might be given in support of the claim that there is a general moral obligation to obey the law do not apply generally enough. They refer to conditions that can, but do not always, exist.

Consider the argument from a "social contract." Taken literally, this argument maintains that each and every one of us is a party to an agreement, either with the rest of us or with those who rule. We have pledged ourselves to obey the law and our pledge binds us. Moreover, it binds us unconditionally: nothing done by the law, or by those in power, can possibly nullify our agreement. For, if the contract can be nullified by, say, outrageously unjust requirements or prohibitions, then the contract does not necessarily bind us. Sufficiently unjust laws would leave us morally free to disobey the law, if that were the morally responsible course of action under the circumstances.

This is incredible – not just because the contract must be construed as unconditional, but more simply because few of us have ever been parties to such an agreement. We have never literally pledged ourselves to obey the law. If we have not done so, then we cannot be bound by such a pledge. This argument does not work, because its conclusion rests on false premises.

A much more plausible suggestion (which avoids the appearance of resting on a fiction) is the argument from fairness. This is the claim that fairness requires us to abide by the law when our turn comes, because we have benefited from others' obedience to the law. However imperfect the laws may be, they bring us palpable benefits, which result from and are dependent on others' obedience. We benefit from the restraints imposed by the law and the coordination it facilitates. Others have the reasonable expectation that we shall reciprocate in kind, and we shall be "free-loaders" unless we do so. We are not simply bound to help others, at risk to our own interests, but to maintain the system that protects us all and that provides, in many cases, additional benefits.

The main difficulty with this argument is that we have no reason to believe that it applies to everyone who falls under the governance of a system of law and to all laws within each system. Why, for example, should we assume that laws promoting aggressive wars of conquest, from which we do not stand to benefit, are covered by such an argument? Resistance to such laws need not deprive us of the benefits to be derived from ordinary criminal laws, which protect us from private aggression; from social regulations, such as traffic laws, which prevent needless suffering; or from laws governing contracts, property, exchange, marriage, and so on. Even if we would personally benefit from our nation's aggressive wars of conquest, which bring cheap resources and slave labor under our collective control, are these not benefits that we should refuse to accept?

But the clearest case to make the general point is provided by laws that secure the exploitation of some class of people, such as laws establishing and protecting chattel slavery. We have no reason to believe that those who are enslaved, but who are still subjected to the laws and can suffer penalties for violating them, are beneficiaries of the system. If they are not beneficiaries of the system, then the argument from fairness simply does not apply to them. And if it does not apply to them, it does not establish a general obligation to obey the law.

Viewed abstractly, it may be puzzling that the idea of a general obligation to obey the law enjoys such widespread credence. Viewed in its social context, however, its prevalence may be less puzzling. For the idea is primarily endorsed by those who see themselves as beneficiaries of the system, and for whom the idea represents a moral commitment to abide by the law even when it is not in *their* personal interest to do so. In this respect, the idea reflects a deliberately conscientious attitude. But it does not seem to reflect a great deal of moral sensitivity, for it totally disregards the position of those who are not beneficiaries of the system. It corresponds to the attitudes expressed by those who speak of "universal suffrage" and "democracy" when they exclude both blacks and women. It is morally myopic.

Sometimes, the idea that we are under a general obligation to obey the law is intended to have narrower scope – to apply just within certain communities, such as those that provide for popular participation in governance. This is surely how the claim is sometimes intended within Great Britain and the United States, for example. But similar considerations apply to these specific cases.

Sometimes, the idea that there is a general obligation to obey the law is backed by a "generalization argument": what would happen if everyone did the same? It is suggested that, if everyone agreed that there is no automatic obligation to obey the law, then legal systems could not survive (because they depend so greatly on voluntary compliance), or at least that law-breaking would be much more widespread, and that laws would be broken when they should be respected.

This argument may be based on a confusion. The claim that there is no automatic obligation to obey the law does *not* imply that there is never any moral obligation to obey the law. Nor does it mean that one is morally free to break the law whenever one wishes to do so. The arguments advanced above assume that there may be an obligation to obey the law, even when the law is morally deficient. So the relevant form of the generalization test is not, "What would happen if everyone believed that there is never any obligation to obey the law?", but rather "What would happen if everyone believed that there is no automatic obligation to obey the law, but rather regarded the law as something that might or might not merit general respect?" If this is the generalization test, then one who uses it as a reason for believing that there is a general obligation to obey the law must think that law and its benefits are exceedingly fragile – that the rule of law cannot survive a conscientious skepticism. The argument even suggests that we must persuade people that they have an automatic obligation to obey the law even if we cannot defend that proposition on its merits. The argument evinces little respect for the conscientiousness and intelligence of ordinary people.

There is need to develop a comprehensive theory of the conditions under which people are morally bound to obey the law. For it does seem reasonable to suppose that one is sometimes bound to abide by social norms that leave something to be desired. But it also appears reasonable to conclude that a legal system does not automatically merit the respect that we might give it by our obedience. Law must earn that respect.

NOTES

For works widely reprinted or available in more than one edition, references are given to standard sections of the texts, such as chapters and paragraphs. The original date of publication is given for historically important works, where known.

1 Moral judgment and the law

1 Thomas Aquinas, *Summa Theologica* (1266–73), I–II, q. 90, art. 4 (p. 747 in *Basic Writings of Saint Thomas Aquinas*, ed. A. C. Pegis [New York: Random House, 1945], vol. 2).

2 John Austin, *The Province of Jurisprudence Determined* (1832), ed. H. L. A. Hart (London: Weidenfeld and Nicolson, 1954), lec. I (p. 24).

3 Aquinas, q. 96, art. 4 (p. 794).

4 *Ibid.*, q. 95, art. 2 (p. 784)

5 *Ibid.*, q. 96, art. 4 (pp. 794–5).

6 See Austin, *Jurisprudence*, lec. I and *passim*.

7 *Ibid.*, lec. VI (pp. 191–2).

8 *Ibid.*, lec. II (p. 37).

9 Immanuel Kant, *Groundwork of the Metaphysics of Morals* (1785), trans. H. J. Paton (London: Hutchinson University Library, 1961); *Critique of Practical Reason* (1788), trans. Lewis White Beck (New York: Liberal Arts Press, 1956).

10 Jeremy Bentham, *An Introduction to the Principles of Morals and Legislation* (1789), ed. J. H. Burns and H. L. A. Hart (London: Athlone Press, 1970), chaps. I–II.

11 William Graham Sumner, *Folkways* (Boston: Ginn and Company, 1907), p. 521.

12 *Ibid.*, sec. 439.

2 Law as social fact

13 Jeremy Bentham, *Of Laws in General*, ed. H. L. A. Hart (London: Athlone Press, 1970); originally published as *The Limits of Jurisprudence Defined*, ed. C. W. Everett (New York: Columbia University Press, 1945).

14 Austin, *Jurisprudence*, lec. I (p. 10); other material in this paragraph is from lectures I, V, and VI.

15 *Ibid.*, lec. V, appended Note (p. 184).

16 Oliver Wendell Holmes, "The Path of the Law," *Harvard Law Review* 10 (1897) 457–78 (paras. 1, 8).

17 William Blackstone, *Commentaries on the Laws of England* (1765–9), vol. I, *Of the Rights of Persons*, Introduction, sec. II. See Austin, *Jurisprudence*, lec. V (pp. 176–80).

18 Bentham, *Laws*, p. 54.

19 H. L. A. Hart, *The Concept of Law* (Oxford: Clarendon Press, 1961), chaps. II–IV. The argument that follows is from chap. III.

20 Austin, *Jurisprudence*, lec. I (pp. 26–33).

21 Austin discusses sovereignty at length in *ibid.*, lec. VI; for criticisms see Hart, *Concept*, chap. IV.

22 Austin, *Jurisprudence*, lec. VI (pp. 216ff).

23 Hart, *Concept*, chaps. V–VI.

24 *Ibid.*, pp. 80–8, 163–80.

3 Morality in law

25 See Hart, *Concept*, pp. 181–95.

26 See Ronald Dworkin, *Taking Rights Seriously* (Cambridge, Mass.: Harvard University Press, 1978), pp. 132–6.

27 This reading of Kelsen was suggested by William Wilcox; see Hans Kelsen, *General Theory of Law and State* (1945), trans. A. Wedberg (New York: Russell & Russell, 1961), pp. 5–13, 49, 410.

28 Holmes, "Path of the Law," paras. 7, 9.

29 Lon L. Fuller, *The Morality of Law* (New Haven and London: Yale University Press, 1964), chap. II.

30 H. L. A. Hart, "Positivism and The Separation of Law and Morals," *Harvard Law Review* 71 (1958) 593–629 and note 25; compare *Concept*, p. 253.

31 Hart, *Concept*, pp. 155–7; see also "Positivism," sec. V.

32 Hart, *Concept*, pp. 156–7.

33 Hart, "Positivism," p. 624.

34 Hart, *Concept*, chap. VII.

35 *Ibid.*, pp. 124–7; see also H. L. A. Hart, "Philosophy of Law, Problems of," in *The Encyclopedia of Philosophy*, ed. P. Edwards (New York: Macmillan and Free Press, 1967), vol. 6, p. 271, and Lon L. Fuller, "Positivism and Fidelity to Law – A Reply to Professor Hart," *Harvard Law Review* 71 (1958) 630–72, sec. VII.

36 Hart, *Concept*, p. 200.

37 115 N.Y. 506, 22 N.E. 188 (1889).

38 Dworkin, *Rights*, chaps. 2–4; Neil MacCormick, *Legal Reasoning and Legal Theory* (Oxford: Clarendon Press, 1978).

39 Kelsen, *General Theory*, pp. 14, 440.

40 Jeremy Bentham, *A Fragment on Government* (1776), Preface, para. 16, in *A Comment on the Commentaries; and A Fragment on Government*, ed. J. H. Burns and H. L. A. Hart (London: Athlone Press, 1977).

41 Dworkin, *Rights*, p. 106.

42 *Ibid.*, pp. 326–7.

43 See *ibid.*, pp. 86–90 and chap. 6.

4 Welfare, justice, and distribution

44 John Stuart Mill, *Utilitarianism* (1861), chap. V, para. 36, in *Essays on Ethics, Religion and Society*, ed. J. M. Robson (Toronto: University of Toronto Press, 1969).

45 Thomas Hobbes, *Leviathan* (1651), ed. K. R. Minogue (London: Dent, 1973).

46 Joseph Butler, "Upon the Love of Our Neighbour" (1726), in *Fifteen Sermons Preached at the Rolls Chapel* (London: Society for Promoting Christian Knowledge, 1970).

47 See William James, "The Moral Philosopher and the Moral Life" (1891), sec. II, in *Essays on Faith and Morals* (New York: World Publishing Company, 1968), pp. 189–98.

48 Aristotle, *Nicomachean Ethics*, Bk. V, in *The Basic Works of Aristotle*, ed. Richard McKeon (New York: Random House, 1941).

49 Mill, *Utilitarianism*, chap. V.

50 Jeremy Bentham, "Anarchical Fallacies," in *The Works of Jeremy Bentham*, ed. J. Bowring (Edinburgh: William Tait, 1838–43), vol. II, p. 501.

51 John Rawls, *A Theory of Justice* (Cambridge, Mass.: Belknap Press, 1971).

52 *Ibid.*, sec. 2.

53 *Ibid.*, p. 60 (this is a "provisional" formulation: for the final version, see pp. 302–3).
54 *Ibid.*, sec. 15.
55 *Ibid.*, secs. 11, 82.
56 *Ibid.*, p. 11.
57 *Ibid.*, pp. 12, 84–8, 136.

5 Legal coercion and moral principle

58 For Kant's ethical theory, summarized in the following four paragraphs, see his *Groundwork of the Metaphysics of Morals*; for its application to punishment, see his *Metaphysical Elements of Justice* (1797), trans. John Ladd (New York: Bobbs-Merrill, 1965). This reading of Kant is suggested by Edmund Pincoffs, *The Rationale of Legal Punishment* (New York: Humanities Press, 1966), chap. I.
59 See Robert Nozick, *Anarchy, State, and Utopia* (New York: Basic Books, 1974), pp. 137–42.
60 Bentham, *Morals and Legislation*, chap. XIII.
61 H. L. A. Hart, "Prolegomenon to the Principles of Punishment," sec. 4, in *Punishment and Responsibility* (New York and Oxford: Oxford University Press, 1968), pp. 18–21.
62 John Rawls, "Two Concepts of Rules," *Philosophical Review* 64 (1955) 3–13.

6 Liberty and law

63 John Stuart Mill, *On Liberty* (1859), ed. Elizabeth Rapaport (Indianapolis: Hackett Publishing Company, 1978), chap. I, para. 9.
64 See, e.g., *ibid.*, chap. IV, art. 12.
65 Mill, *Utilitarianism*, chap. II, paras. 1–10; *Liberty*, chap. III.
66 Dworkin, *Rights*, pp. 188–92.
67 Patrick Devlin, *The Enforcement of Morals* (London: Oxford University Press, 1965), esp. chap. I.
68 Mill, *Utilitarianism*, chap. V, para. 14.
69 Mill, *Liberty*, chap. I, para. 11.
70 Devlin, *Enforcement*, pp. 14–18.
71 Plato, *The Republic*, trans. G. M. A. Grube (Indianapolis: Hackett Publishing Company, 1973).

72 Mill, *Liberty*, chap. III, para. 1 (for Mill's arguments, see chap. II).
73 *Ibid.*, chap. III, para. 1.

7 The rule of law
74 Bentham, *Fragment*, Preface, para. 16.

BIBLIOGRAPHY

This is a brief list of suggested further readings, organized around the chapters of this text. Some items are reprinted, as indicated, in general anthologies on law and philosophy, a list of which is appended. (Anthologies on more specific topics are included in the chapter listings.) Full information on a work cited more than once is given in the first entry.

1 Moral judgment and the law

Ayer, A. J., "On the Analysis of Moral Judgements," in *Philosophical Essays* (London: Macmillan, 1954), pp. 231–49. [Values are independent of facts.]

Brandt, Richard B., *Ethical Theory* (Englewood Cliffs, N.J.: Prentice-Hall, 1959), chaps. 1–11. [On the justifiability of moral judgments.]

Hare, R. M., *The Language of Morals* (Oxford: Oxford University Press, 1952). [Individualistic relativism.]

Hare, R. M., *Freedom and Reason* (Oxford: Clarendon Press, 1963).

Hare, R. M., *Moral Thinking* (Oxford: Clarendon Press, 1981).

Harman, Gilbert, "Moral Relativism Defended," *Philosophical Review* 84 (1975) 3–32.

Harman, Gilbert, *The Nature of Morality* (New York: Oxford University Press, 1977).

Harman, Gilbert, "Relativistic Ethics: Morality as Politics," *Midwest Studies in Philosophy* 3 (1978) 109–12.

Herskovits, Melville, *Cultural Anthropology* (New York: Knopf, 1955), chap. 19 [same as *Man and His Works* (New York: Knopf, 1948), chap. 5]. [Social relativism.]

Mackie, J. L., *Ethics: Inventing Right and Wrong* (Harmondsworth: Penguin Books, 1977).

Rawls, John, "Outline of a Decision Procedure for Ethics," *Philosophical Review* 60 (1951) 177–97. [A theory of justification. Repr. in Thomson and Dworkin (below).]

Stevenson, Charles L., *Ethics and Language* (New Haven: Yale University Press, 1944). [The emotive theory of ethics.]

Sumner, William Graham, *Folkways* (Boston: Ginn and Company, 1907). [Social relativism.]

Thomson, Judith J., and Gerald Dworkin, eds., *Ethics* (London: Harper & Row, 1968).

Urmson, J. O., *The Emotive Theory of Ethics* (London: Hutchinson University Library, 1968).

Wellman, Carl, "The Ethical Implications of Cultural Relativity," *Journal of Philosophy* 60 (1963) 169–84.

2 Law as social fact

Austin, John, *The Province of Jurisprudence Determined*, ed. H. L. A. Hart (London: Weidenfeld and Nicolson, 1954). [Repr. in Christie; excerpts in Feinberg and Gross, Golding, Kent.]

Bentham, Jeremy, *Of Laws in General*, ed. H. L. A. Hart (London: Athlone Press, 1970).

Dworkin, Ronald, *Taking Rights Seriously* (Cambridge, Mass.: Harvard University Press, 1978), chaps. 1–3. [Chap. 2 repr. in Dworkin, Feinberg and Gross, Summers, *Essays.*]

Golding, Martin P., *Philosophy of Law* (Englewood Cliffs, N.J.: Prentice-Hall, 1975), chaps. 1–2.

Gray, John Chipman, *The Nature and Sources of the Law* (Boston: Beacon Press, 1963), chap. IV. [Law is made by courts. Repr. in Christie, Feinberg and Gross.]

Hart, H. L. A., *The Concept of Law* (Oxford: Clarendon Press,1961).

Hart, H. L. A., "Philosophy of Law, Problems of," in *The Encyclopedia of Philosophy*, ed. P. Edwards (New York: Macmillan and Free Press, 1967), vol. 6, pp. 264–76. [Repr. in Feinberg and Gross.]

Holmes, Oliver Wendell, "The Path of the Law," *Harvard Law Review* 10 (1897) 457–78. [Repr. in Golding, Henson, Kent.]

Kelsen, Hans, *General Theory of Law and State*, trans. A. Wedberg (New York: Russell & Russell, 1961). [Excerpts repr. in Christie.]

MacCormick, Neil, *Legal Reasoning and Legal Theory* (Oxford: Clarendon Press, 1978).

MacCormick, Neil, *H. L. A. Hart* (Stanford: Stanford University Press, 1981).

Raz, Joseph, *The Concept of a Legal System* (Oxford: Clarendon Press, 1970).

Raz, Joseph, *The Authority of Law* (Oxford: Clarendon Press, 1979), part II.

3 Morality in law

Aquinas, Thomas, "Treatise on Law," in *The Summa Theologica of Saint Thomas Aquinas*, trans. Fathers of the English Dominican Province (London: Washbourne, 1912–15), vol. 7. [Excerpts repr. in Christie, Feinberg and Gross, Golding.]

Dworkin, *Taking Rights Seriously*. [Chap. 8 repr. in Feinberg and Gross, Kipnis.]

Fuller, Lon L., "Positivism and Fidelity to Law – A Reply to Professor Hart," *Harvard Law Review* 71 (1958) 630–72. [Repr. in Feinberg and Gross.]

Fuller, Lon L., *The Morality of Law*, Revised Edition (New Haven: Yale University Press, 1969).

Georgia Law Review 11 (September 1977), Jurisprudence Symposium. [Papers by Hart, Dworkin and others.]

Golding, *Philosophy of Law*, chaps. 2, 6.

Hart, H. L. A., "Positivism and the Separation of Law and Morals," *Harvard Law Review* 71 (1958) 593–629. [Repr. in Dworkin, Feinberg and Gross, Kent.]

Hart, *The Concept of Law*, chap. IX.

Lyons, David, "On Formal Justice," *Cornell Law Review* 58 (1973) 833–61.

Lyons, David, "Moral Aspects of Legal Theory," *Midwest Studies in Philosophy* 7 (1982) 223–54.

Morawetz, Thomas, *The Philosophy of Law* (New York: Macmillan, 1980), chaps. 1–2.

Raz, *The Authority of Law*, parts II–III.

Richards, David A. J., *The Moral Criticism of Law* (Encino and Belmont, Ca.: Dickenson, 1977), chaps. 1–2.

4 Welfare, justice, and distribution

Blocker, H. Gene, and Elizabeth H. Smith, eds., *John Rawls's Theory of Social Justice* (Athens, Ohio: Ohio University Press, 1980). [A collection of critical studies.]

Brandt, Richard B., *A Theory of the Good and the Right* (Oxford: Clarendon Press, 1979). [A version of utilitarianism.]

Brandt, *Ethical Theory*, chaps. 12–17.

Daniels, Norman, ed., *Reading Rawls* (Oxford: Blackwell, 1975). [A collection of critical studies.]

Dworkin, Ronald, "What is Equality?", *Philosophy & Public Affairs* 10 (1981) 185–246, 283–345.

Feinberg, Joel, *Social Philosophy* (Englewood Cliffs, N.J.: Prentice-Hall, 1973), chap. 7.

Hart, *The Concept of Law*, chap. VIII.

Held, Virginia, ed., *Property, Profits, and Economic Justice* (Belmont, Ca.: Wadsworth, 1980). [A collection of readings.]

Hofstra Law Review 8 (Spring 1980), Symposium on Efficiency as a Legal Concern. [Papers by Dworkin and others on the economic counterpart to utilitarianism.]

Lyons, David, "Mill's Theory of Justice," in *Values and Morals*, ed. A. I. Goldman and J. Kim (Dordrecht: Reidel, 1978), pp. 1–20.

Lyons, David, "Utility and Rights," in *Ethics, Economics, and the Law: NOMOS XXIV*, ed. J. R. Pennock and J. W. Chapman (New York: New York University Press, 1982), pp. 107–38.

Lyons, David, ed., *Rights* (Belmont, Ca.: Wadsworth, 1979). [A collection of contemporary studies.]

Mill, John Stuart, *Utilitarianism* (many editions). [Chap. V repr. in Feinberg and Gross.]

Nozick, Robert, *Anarchy, State, and Utopia* (New York: Basic Books, 1974), esp. chap. 7.

Rawls, John, *A Theory of Justice* (Cambridge, Mass.: Belknap Press, 1971).

Rescher, Nicholas, *Distributive Justice* (Indianapolis: Bobbs-Merrill, 1966). [Excerpts repr. in Feinberg and Gross.]

Sartorius, Rolf, *Individual Conduct and Social Norms* (Encino and Belmont, Ca.: Dickenson, 1975). [A utilitarian view.]

Smart, J. J. C., and Bernard Williams, *Utilitarianism, For and Against* (Cambridge: Cambridge University Press, 1973).

Sterba, James, ed., *Justice* (Belmont, Ca.: Wadsworth, 1980). [A collection of readings.]

5 Legal coercion and moral principle

Brandt, *Ethical Theory*, chaps. 18–20.

Ezorsky, Gertrude, ed., *Philosophical Perspectives on Punishment*

(Albany: State University of New York Press, 1972). [A collection of readings.]

Feinberg, Joel, *Doing and Deserving* (Princeton: Princeton University Press, 1970).

Golding, *Philosophy of Law*, chaps. 4–5.

Hart, H. L. A., *Punishment and Responsibility* (New York and Oxford: Oxford University Press, 1968).

McCloskey, H. J., "A Non-Utilitarian Approach to Punishment," *Inquiry* 8 (1965) 249–63. [Repr. in Ezorsky (above), Feinberg and Gross, Murphy (below).]

Morawetz, *The Philosophy of Law*, chap. 4.

Morris, Herbert, "Persons and Punishment," *Monist* 52 (1968) 475–501. [Repr. in Ezorsky (above), Feinberg and Gross, Murphy (below).]

Murphy, Jeffrie G., ed., *Punishment and Rehabilitation* (Belmont, Ca.: Wadsworth, 1973). [A collection of readings.]

Nozick, Robert, *Philosophical Explanations* (Cambridge, Mass.: Belknap Press, 1981), pp. 363–97.

Pennock, J. R., and J. W. Chapman, eds., *Coercion: NOMOS XIV* (Chicago: Aldine-Atherton, 1972). [A collection of papers.]

Pincoffs, Edmund, *The Rationale of Legal Punishment* (New York: Humanities Press, 1966). [Chap. I repr. in Feinberg and Gross.]

Rawls, John, "Two Concepts of Rules," *Philosophical Review* 64 (1955) 3–32. [Repr. in Thomson and Dworkin; excerpts repr. in Ezorsky (above), Feinberg and Gross, Murphy (above).]

Richards, *The Moral Criticism of Law*, chaps. 5–6.

6 Liberty and law

Berger, Fred R., ed., *Freedom of Expression* (Belmont, Ca.: Wadsworth, 1980). [A collection of readings.]

Devlin, Patrick, *The Enforcement of Morals* (London: Oxford University Press, 1965). [Chap. I repr. in Dworkin and in Wasserstrom (below).]

Dworkin, Gerald, "Paternalism," in Wasserstrom (below), pp. 107–26. [Repr. in Feinberg and Gross.]

Dworkin, *Taking Rights Seriously*, chaps. 10–11.

Feinberg, Joel, "Limits to the Free Expression of Opinion," in Feinberg and Gross, pp. 191–206.

Feinberg, Joel, *Rights, Justice, and the Bounds of Liberty* (Princeton: Princeton University Press, 1980).

Feinberg, *Social Philosophy*, chaps. 1–3.

Golding, *Philosophy of Law*, chap. 3.

Hart, H. L. A., *Law, Liberty, and Morality* (Stanford: Stanford University Press, 1963).

Lyons, David, "Liberty and Harm to Others," *Canadian Journal of Philosophy*, suppl. vol. V (1979) 1–19.

Mill, John Stuart, *On Liberty* (many editions). [Chap. II repr. in Berger (above), Feinberg and Gross; chap. IV repr. in Wasserstrom (below).]

Morawetz, *The Philosophy of Law*, chap. 3.

Nozick, *Anarchy, State, and Utopia*. [A libertarian theory.]

Richards, *The Moral Criticism of Law*, chap. 3.

Scanlon, Thomas, "A Theory of Freedom of Expression," *Philosophy & Public Affairs* 1 (1972) 204–26. [Repr. in Dworkin.]

Wasserstrom, Richard A., ed., *Morality and the Law* (Belmont, Ca.: Wadsworth, 1971). [A collection of readings.]

7 The rule of law

Dworkin, *Taking Rights Seriously*, chap. 8. [Repr. in Feinberg and Gross.]

Golding, *Philosophy of Law*, chap. 6.

Nelson, William N., *On Justifying Democracy* (London: Routledge & Kegan Paul, 1980).

Pennock, J. R., and J. W. Chapman, eds., *Due Process: NOMOS XVIII* (New York: New York University Press, 1977). [A collection of papers.]

Pennock, J. R., and J. W. Chapman, eds., *Participation in Politics: NOMOS XVI* (New York: Lieber-Atherton, 1975). [A collection of papers.]

Pennock, J. R., and J. W. Chapman, eds., *Political and Legal Obligation: NOMOS XII* (New York: Atherton, 1970). [A collection of papers.]

Plato, *The Crito*. [The classic social contract argument.]

Rawls, *A Theory of Justice*, secs. 37–8, 51–9.

Raz, *The Authority of Law*, parts I and IV.

Simmons, A. John, *Moral Principles and Political Obligations* (Princeton: Princeton University Press, 1979).

Smith, M. B. E., "Is There a Prima Facie Obligation to Obey the Law?", *Yale Law Journal* 82 (1973) 950–76. [Repr. in Feinberg and Gross.]

Summers, Robert S., "Evaluating and Improving Legal Processes – A Plea for 'Process Values'," *Cornell Law Review* 60 (1974) 1–51.

Wasserstrom, Richard A., "The Obligation to Obey the Law," *UCLA Law Review* 10 (1963) 780–807. [Repr. in Summers, *Essays*.]

Woozley, A. D., *Law and Obedience: The Arguments of Plato's Crito* (Chapel Hill: University of North Carolina Press, 1979).

Some general anthologies

Christie, George C., *Jurisprudence* (St Paul: West, 1973). [Extensive readings from historically important philosophers.]

Dworkin, Ronald, *The Philosophy of Law* (Oxford: Oxford University Press, 1977).

Feinberg, Joel, and Hyman Gross, *Philosophy of Law*, Second Edition (Belmont, Ca.: Wadsworth, 1980). [Readings on law, liberty, justice, responsibility, and punishment.]

Golding, Martin P., *The Nature of Law* (New York: Random House, 1966).

Henson, Ray D., *Landmarks of Law* (Boston: Beacon Press, 1960).

Kent, Edward Allen, *Law and Philosophy* (New York: Appleton-Century-Crofts, 1970).

Kipnis, Kenneth, *Philosophical Issues in Law* (Englewood Cliffs, N.J.: Prentice-Hall, 1977).

Summers, Robert S., *Essays in Legal Philosophy* (Oxford: Blackwell, 1968).

Summers, Robert S., *More Essays in Legal Philosophy* (Berkeley and Los Angeles: University of California Press, 1971).

INDEX